THE
MUMMIES
OF
EGYPT

JOHN J. DAVIS

The Story of Egyptian Mummies

BMH BOOKS
P.O. BOX 544
WINONA LAKE, INDIANA 46590

To
Mrs. Janet Ward

Acknowledgements

The author wishes to express special appreciation to the following individuals who have made significant contributions to the preparation of this volume.

Robert D. Ibach, Jr., Director of Libraries; Associate Professor of Old Testament and Archaeology, Grace College and Grace Theological Seminary, who read the manuscript and made many helpful suggestions.

Donald L. Fowler, Professor of Old Testament and Hebrew, Grace Theological Seminary, who evaluated sections of the book resulting in numerous improvements.

Ken Herman, Manager and Director of Production, BMH Printing, who worked so diligently and creatively on the layout of the book.

Scott Boerckel, post-graduate Student at Grace Theological Seminary, who read the manuscript and suggested worthwhile changes.

Jim Coakley, post-graduate student at Grace Theological Seminary, who prepared the indices.

Ella Male and Frankie Putney who assisted in the typing of the manuscript.

Charles W. Turner, Executive Editor and General Manager, BMH Productions, for his cooperation and encouragement in the entire project.

To all the students who have studied archaeology with the author the past 22 years goes a special expression of gratitude. It has been their interest and enthusiasm for the subject which has prompted this effort.

Table of Contents

List of Photo Credits 2

Foreword 7

1. The Great Discoveries 9
   Tomb Curses
   The Early Explorers

2. The Way of Death 23
   Concepts of After-Life
   The Funerary Ritual

3. Tombs, Temples and Pyramids 41
   The Tomb Robbers
   The Early Years
   The Old Kingdom
   Tombs of the Middle and New Kingdoms
   Graeco-Roman Tombs

4. Embalmers and Mummies 71
   The Origin of Mummification
   The Methods of Mummification
   Coffins
   Mummification of Animals
   Significant Burial Objects

5. New Light on Old Bones 107
   The Manchester Project
   Mummy Powder Medicine

6. Mummification and the Bible 119
   Physicians and Embalmers
   Great Faith

Documentation 129

Bibliography 134

Indices 140

Foreword

Interest in the ancient world, especially in Egyptian studies, continues unabated. The headlines that greet each new find testify to the intense interest around the world in the study of ancient history. On a recent trip to a famous museum, I noticed a multitude of volumes concerning ancient Egypt on sale in the museum bookstore, reflecting such interest. The emergence of this volume by Dr. Davis comes as an appropriate response to an ever-growing inquisitiveness regarding the subject of death and burial, generally, and the practices of the Egyptians, specifically.

Dr. Davis has managed to avoid several major pitfalls which have characterized much of the material written on ancient Egypt. Happily, the minutae and obscurantism that so often attends scholarly work is unattested here. Equally important, at the opposite extremity, is that this volume is neither sensationalist nor superficial even though the subject matter itself is of sensational interest. When it is presented with clarity and lucidity by a gifted writer, the result is as informative as it is entertaining.

This book presents a study of burial techniques and traditions throughout Egypt's long history. This linear approach to burial practices is, therefore, accompanied with a wealth of data on Egyptian history and religion, and interfaces with the ancient Hebrews. These features make the volume of interest to both antiquarians and students of the Old Testament.

The book is superbly illustrated, well-documented, and represents the work of the most modern techniques for examining mummies. Coming from the pen of an Old Testament scholar and veteran archaeologist who has specialized in tombs, the author is well-qualified to render the synthetical treatment of ancient burial practices in Egypt. The book is equally valuable to pastors, teachers, and students of the Bible. I heartily recommend it to the reading public everywhere.

Donald L. Fowler, Th.D.

1 The Great Discoveries

Ancient Egypt with her temples, kings, priests and mummies continues to fascinate the modern mind. Some might consider preoccupation with the study of death a rather morbid activity, but confrontation with the Egyptians' approach to death and burial quickly disspells such notions. Perhaps no other ancient culture has received more attention than the ancient Egyptians because of their unique ideas of an after-life, and the methods by which they preserved the body for it.

While this subject has been thoroughly discussed and analyzed from the standpoint of competent scholarship, many popular articles continue to be written which border on the fanciful and the extravagant. Significant discoveries made in Egypt have often been described with an air of mystery and intrigue by journalists. The uncovering of tombs and the burial chambers of the royal kings has been especially subject to this type of literary treatment.

For example, a radio drama focusing on the discoveries

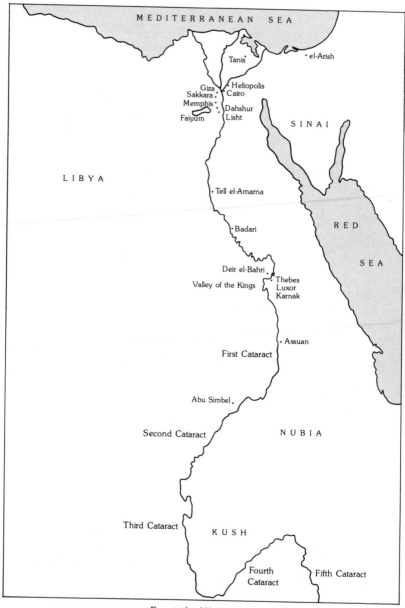

Egypt, the Nile Valley

of Archibald Jones and his archaeological team in the desert sands of Egypt might go something like this. "After weeks of hard work, Professor Jones finally came across an unopened tomb entrance. A great air of excitement captivated the imagination of the workers and restraint was needed to keep them from approaching their task with too much enthusiasm which would inevitably lead to reckless methodology. Nonetheless, after arduous effort the door of the tomb, far below the surface of the ground, was opened and the chief archaeologist along with his assistant entered with lanterns. They were the first men to see the inside of the tomb since its original sealing more than 3000 years ago. Even with the dim light of their lanterns they were made spellbound by the beauty of the paintings on the walls and the statues which lined the small chambers to either side."

"Even more spectacular, was the final burial chamber at the end of the passage way. There, gold statues, ivory inlaid boxes, with a host of beautifully carved alabaster objects were seen stacked around the walls of the chamber. In the center of the room was a large granite sarcophagus. After the objects were carefully photographed and recorded, the archaeologist continued his work. The lid of the large black sarcophagus had to be lifted and this was done with great care by ten of his workers who had joined him in the main chamber. Upon opening the lid, they gazed upon the beautiful anthropoid coffin of one individual."

"Carefully the coffin was lifted out of the large sarcophagus and placed on the table in the chamber designed to support the body. When this was accomplished, the workers were released for the remainder of the day and Professor Jones remained alone in the tomb. Fascinated by the implications of this discovery, he found himself unable to break away from the tomb and decided to explore further the mummy which he had just discovered. Unwrapping the mummy was an extremely tedious task, however. It was not until late in the night that top half of the mummy was finally unwrapped and exposed to the air for the first time in three thousand years."

"Weary from such effort, he decided to sit down and rest on the other side of the chamber. While seated, he made a few notes and observations concerning the work of the previous hours. As he was writing, a large clap of thunder was heard outside and lightning flashed across the dark skies. Through the opening in the tomb at the other end of the chamber he could see the black clouds of an unexpected Egyptian storm. The roaring thunder was reminiscent of the roar of the Egyptian lion goddess, perhaps in disapproval of the proceedings. Nonetheless, Archibald continued his work and after making a final notation on the page, he looked up and as he did he found himself staring into the now open eyes and haunting grin of the mummy. . ."

Space prevents us from completing this intriguing tale, but it exemplifies the type of literary treatment afforded the mummies of ancient Egypt. While such material provides interesting reading, it hardly aids in understanding burial customs and in particular, mummification practices of ancient Egypt.

Tomb Curses

Another fascinating topic with regard to Egypt's ancient tombs has to do with the curse placed on those who entered the sacred chambers. In an edition of the *Dorsett Evening Echo*, published in Great Britain, the following headline appeared in bold type: "Professor Dies While Handling Death Statue." The reference was to the well-known British Egyptologist, Walter Emery, who died at age 67. According to the report, the professor discovered the statue of the Egyptian god of death (Osiris), and was handling it when he collapsed with cerebral thrombosis. The discovery of the statue,

This statue of the Eighteenth Dynasty's Thutmoses III was discovered at Karnak.
Photo by the author.

combined with the presumed curses placed on those desecrating ancient tombs, was supposed to have been the cause of death. The writer of the article, of course, failed to note for his readers that Professor Emery had handled hundreds of such statues on previous occasions from a variety of tombs. That death should strike him at this point was nothing more than coincidental.

Other attempts to give credibility to the curses of Egypt's ancient tombs have been widespread. These were fueled by a 1924 suicide note written by British Egyptologist Hugh Evelyn-White in his own blood just before he hanged himself. Since he was among the first to enter the tomb of Tutankhamun after its discovery in November 1922, writers immediately associated his tragic death with "the Pharaonic curse." Other members of Howard Carter's team also passed away shortly after the tomb's discovery. What was not revealed, however, is that some of these individuals were in poor health and advanced age when they went to Egypt.

Dr. Caroline Stenger-Philippe, a French physician, has recently argued that at least six of the deaths can be traced to an allergic reaction to fungi or mold which grew in the air-tight chambers of the tomb. According to Stenger-Philippe, in a doctoral thesis presented to the Strasbourg University School of Medicine, the victims contracted allergic alveolitis, a severe inflamation of the tiny air chambers in the lungs, and died of pulmonary insufficiency.

The mold which later became organic dust originated from the fruits and vegetables along with other organic materials which had been placed in the tomb to nourish the deceased Pharaoh. She pointed out that when explorers entered these tombs they paid little attention to the pink, gray and green patches of fungi on the walls. Such an oversight turned out to be fatal in their cases.

The Early Explorers

The various accounts of tomb robbing and exploitation of Egyptian mummies by the ancient Egyptians themselves, modern Arabs and European explorers would rival any murder mystery in complexity and emotional intrigue. The stories about the ancient tomb robbers will be discussed later in this volume. Here however, the focus is upon the modern explorers and their account of tomb discoveries.

The fascination with the monuments of ancient Egypt existed among the Greeks and brought many travellers to the land of Egypt as a result. Like some of today's tourists, they left their names and thoughts scratched on the tombs and monuments. Defacement of Egypt's precious monuments can also be credited to the ancient Egyptian tourists as well.

> Indeed, ancient Egyptian tourists' graffiti often disfigured - and neglect certainly destroyed - so many monuments that one of Ramesses II's sons, Khaemwese, spent much of his time trying to restore them. He seems to have been a withdrawn, melancholy person, liking nothing better than to wander for hours round the Memphis necropolis reading the inscriptions on the tombs and temple walls.[1]

During the eighteenth and early nineteenth centuries, a significant number of "explorers" were found wandering the desert sands of Egypt in search of tombs and antiquities. Their goal was treasure hunting and their methods were patently unscientific and, in many cases, destructive. Some of these explorers were not even subtle about their intention. Giovanni Battista Belzoni confessed the following: "The purpose of my researches was to rob the Egyptians of their papyri; of which I found a few hidden in their breasts under their arms, in the space above the knees, or on the legs, and covered by the numerous folds of cloth, that envelope the mummy."[2]

Very brutal methods were utilized to recover tomb

The exposed head of a 3000-year-old mummy named Djed-Khons-Iwef-Ankh with eyelashes and eyebrows intact. *Photograph by Mary Beth Camp. Courtesy of the Cleveland Health Education Museum and St. Luke's Hospital.*

materials. Having located the entrance to one royal tomb in the western Valley of the Kings, Belzoni proceeded to open it with a battering ram made of two palm logs.[3] His description of his experience in opening royal tombs is most fascinating.

Of some of these tombs many persons could not withstand the suffocating air which often causes fainting. A vast quantity of dust rises, so fine that it enters into the throat and nostrils and chokes the nose and mouth to such a degree, that it requires great power of lungs to resist it and the strong effluvia of the mummies. This is not all; the entry or passage where the bodies are is roughly cut in the rocks, and the falling sand from the upper part of the ceiling of the passage causes it to be nearly filled up. In some places there is not more than a vacancy of a foot left, which you must contrive to pass through in a creeping posture like a snail, on pointed and keen stones that cut like glass.[4]

The destruction of valuable archaeological materials within the tomb was widespread as a result of these clandestine explorations. Belzoni records the following:

. . . I sought a resting place, found one, and contrived to sit; but when my weight bore on the body of an Egyptian, it crushed like a bandbox. I naturally had recourse to my hands to sustain my weight, but they found no better support; so that I sunk altogether among the broken mummies with a crash of bones, rags, and wooden cases, which raised such a dust as to keep me motionless for a quarter of an hour, waiting until it subsided again. I could not remove from the place, however, without increasing it, and every step I took I crushed a mummy in some part or other. Once I was conducted from such a place to another resembling it, through a passage of about 20 feet in length, and no wider than that a body could be forced through. It was choked with mummies, and I could not pass without putting my face in contact with that of some decayed Egyptian; but as the passage inclined downward, my own weight helped me on; however, I could not avoid being covered with bones, legs, arms, and heads rolling from above. Thus I proceeded from one case to another, all full of mummies piled up in various ways, some standing, some lying, and some on their heads.[5]

Tomb robbing by Arab villagers near the Valley of the Kings was a major enterprise involving hundreds of people and it continued over a lengthy period of time. Happily, however, the great French Egyptologist, Gaston Maspero, encountered some hitherto unknown relics that were being sold privately. He immediately suspected that a new cache of antiquities had been found in Egypt and were being marketed to wealthy Europeans. Launching a brilliant piece of detective

Entrance to one of the royal tombs in Thebes. *Photo by the author.*

work, he found the location of the tomb and actually rescued dozens of mummies and other valuable artifacts from the Eighteenth through the Twenty-first Dynasties.

After numerous investigations and back-alley inquiries, he discovered that the principal marketers of the antiquities were two brothers living in the village of Qurneh, near the Valley of the Kings. Even though he was aware that Arabs had discovered an unknown royal tomb of the Twenty-first Dynasty in 1878, it was not until June 25, 1881 that the exact location was discovered.

This turned out to be one of the most important Egyptian archaeological discoveries in history. Today it is referred to as "Deir el Bahri cache." The location of the treasure was in the tomb of Queen Inhapy, which lay behind the Deir el Bahri Temple on the west bank at Thebes. Because of extensive tomb robbery and destruction during the latter part of the twelfth century B.C., a group of priests gathered the remaining mummies and objects from the various tombs and secretly reburied them in the tomb of Queen Inhapy. Those who entered the tomb 3000 years later described the bodies as having been stacked like logs.

Gaston Maspero was among those who entered the tomb and saw the mummies. His description is worth noting:

. . . A little further on was a coffin of the Seventeenth Dynasty style, then the Queen Tiuhathor Henttaui, then Seti I. Beside the coffins and scattered on the ground were wooden funerary statuettes, canopic jars, bronze libation vases, and at the back in corner angle made by the passage as it turned northward was the funeral tent of Queen Isiemkheb bent and crumbled like a valueless object which a priest in a hurry to get out had thrown carelessly into a corner. The entire length of the main passage was similarly obstructed and disordered: It was necessary to advance on all fours not knowing where one was putting hands and feet. The coffins and the mummies rapidly glimpsed by the light of candle bore historic names, Amenhetep I, Thuthmoses II, Inche near the steps, Ahmose I and son Siamun, Sequenre,

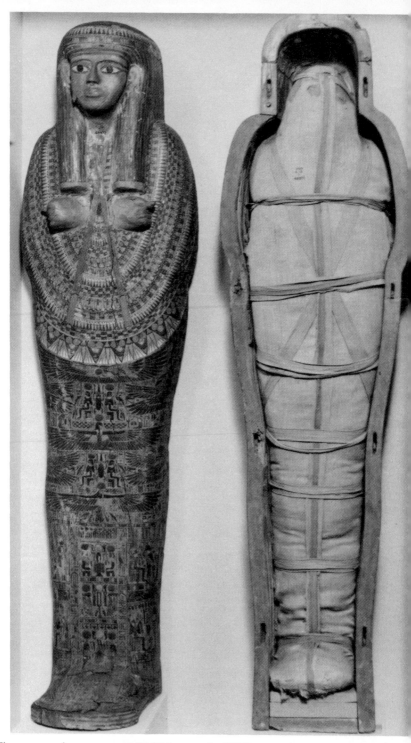

The mummy of a woman aged 35-48 dating to the XXI Dynasty. *Courtesy the British Museum*

Queen Ahotpe, Ahmose, Nefertari and others. The chamber at the end was the height of confusion, but it was possible to see at first glance that the style of the Twentieth Dynasty predominated. Mohammed Ahamed Abd-er-Rassouls's report which had at first seemed exaggerated hardly expressed the truth: where I had expected to find one or two minor kings, the Arabs had dug up a vault full of Pharaohs and what Pharaohs! . . . I still ask myself if it is true and if I am dreaming when I see and touch the bodies of all these people when we never thought to know more than their names.[6]

This was not the end of such spectacular discoveries however. In 1898, V. Loret, an Egyptologist made his own discovery of another royal cache in the tomb of Amenhotep II in the Valley of the Kings. The mummies of missing Pharaohs in the Deir el Bahri cache were located here. Among the kings were Merenptah, Thuthmoses IV, and Amenhotep III. The mummy of Amenhotep II remained in the tomb while the others were taken to Cairo. Unfortunately, two years later tomb guards were overpowered by robbers and the mummy of Amenhotep II was stripped of its valuable antiquities.[7]

Without question, however, one of the most widely publicized discoveries was made in 1922 by Howard Carter and his team. The location of the tomb of Tutankhamun constitutes one of the more significant archaeological events because his is the only nearly-intact royal burial from the first Twenty-Dynasties that has ever been found. Evidence indicates, however, that it had been entered twice by tomb robbers. The burial was especially significant because it was one of the very few primary royal burials which contained a complete repertoire of funerary equipment. Also important to scholars was the opportunity to study the actual body of Tutankhamun in order to clarify very complex questions concerning family relationships during the Eighteenth Dynasty in Egypt.

While discovery of ancient Egyptian tombs was not always

the result of carefully designed archaeological work, nonetheless, the surviving bodies of the kings provide remarkable information about their life, death and achievements, a matter to be explored more fully in Chapter 5 of this volume.

The unopened tombs of royal princes and other important political figures continue to be discovered. Happily, however, the discoveries are a result of carefully disciplined excavation. One can only speculate at the splendor that must have characterized the original burials of kings like Thuthmoses III and Ramses II.

2 The Way of Death

For most of their history the Egyptians possessed a well-defined concept of an after-life. How this originated is not known, but based on anthropological studies from other parts of the world, it is clear they were not alone in such beliefs.

Perhaps such ideas are more intuitive in nature than acquired or discovered. If mankind was created in the image and likeness of God as the Bible affirms (Gen. 1:26), then his universal inclination toward unending existence would be an integral part of his nature. Widely separated cultures consistently prepare for such experience as evidenced by their burial assemblages.

That such unending existence is a natural consequence of human intuition is illustrated by the genuine inability of an individual to conceive of his demise and subsequent non-existence. If the reader would like an interesting experience, he should withdraw to a completely secluded and quiet place, then endeavor to picture his death and following non-

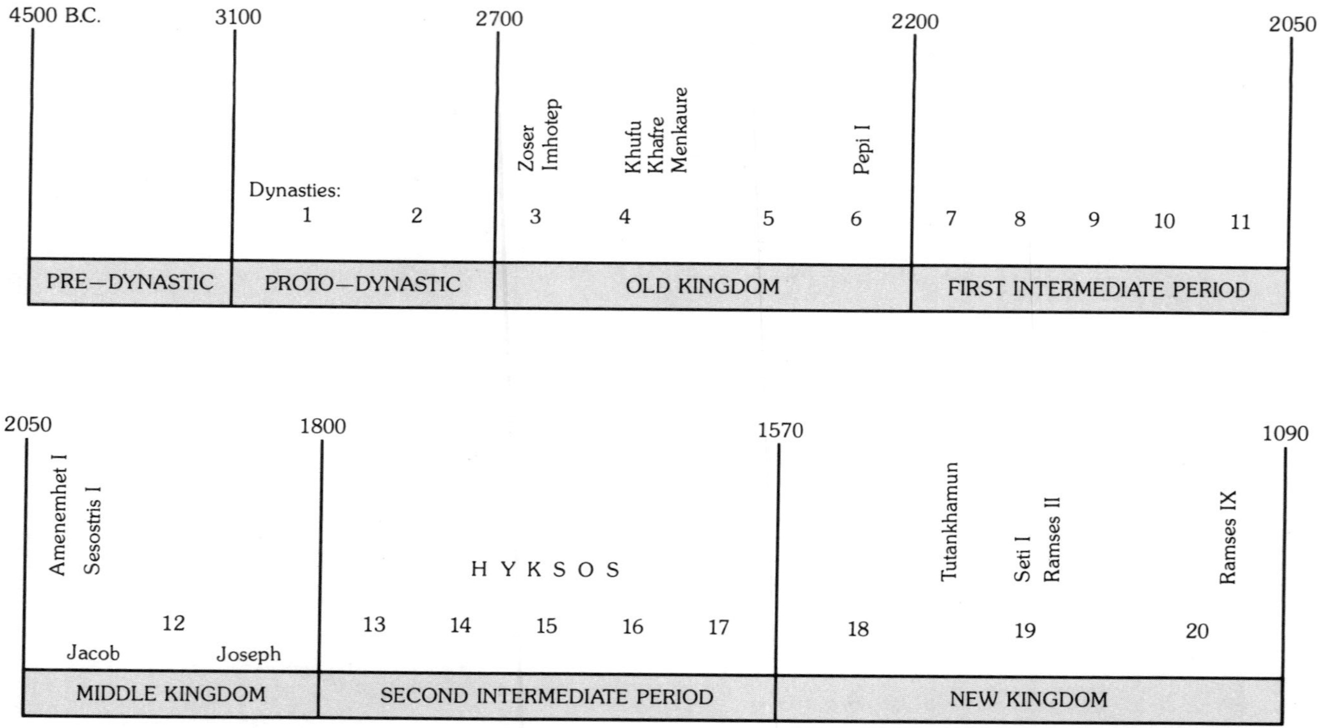

PRE—DYNASTIC

4500 B.C.

3100

PROTO—DYNASTIC

Dynasties: 1 2

2700

OLD KINGDOM

3 Zoser
   Imhotep

4 Khufu
   Khafre
   Menkaure

5

6 Pepi I

2200

FIRST INTERMEDIATE PERIOD

7 8 9 10 11

2050

2050

MIDDLE KINGDOM

Amenemhet I
Sesostris I

12

Jacob   Joseph

1800

SECOND INTERMEDIATE PERIOD

13 14 15 16 17

H Y K S O S

1570

NEW KINGDOM

18

Tutankhamun

19 Seti I
    Ramses II

20 Ramses IX

1090

existence. Attempting to envision one's lack of existence is, for most, a very disconcerting experience. In fact, many have argued that it is impossible.

The normal desires of human life appear to extend beyond mere physical existence and such were the expectations of the ancient Egyptians who clearly believed in a conscious after-life. The evidence for this belief is the fact that they did as much for their dead as they did for many of their living rulers and even their gods.

Deir el-Bahri's magnificent temples, the awesome hypostyle hall at Karnak and the great colonnade at Luxor are just a few examples of the tremendous effort that went into the preparation for death and the life to follow. The splendid treasures found in the burial chambers of kings and nobles not only memorialized their past, but were considered necessary for a happy future life.

Concepts of After-Life

The Egyptian concepts of death and the after-life were very physically oriented. In the light of this, it would appear that the Egyptians had two fundamental reasons why they were so careful in preserving the human body after death: first, they wanted to guarantee effective functions of the body in the land beyond the sunset and second, they wanted to assure continued identity of the individual.

It was believed that after death, the Ba (translated "soul" by some) traveled with the sun on its nightly journey through the underworld, then returned in the morning to the deceased. The body of the individual was its dwelling place and, therefore, had to be preserved. Furthermore, for the Ba to find its legitimate home, it had to be able to identify the body from which it had come. The Egyptian believed that careful embalming would guarantee these goals.

In order that this "spirit" or "soul" might have appropriate sustenance, food and other offerings were placed in the tomb. Provision for continued life was also made by the magical power of tomb paintings.

The concept of life after death went through various changes and revisions throughout Egyptian history. As early as the pre-Dynastic period (c. 4500-3100 B.C.), there was some sort of belief in an after-life as demonstrated by the type of assemblages placed with the dead. Such funerary gifts consisted of pottery vessels, beads, flint tools, and other objects of possible amuletic value.

Pre-Dynastic bodies were largely placed in pits and were often wrapped in goatskins or woven matting. Originally, these burial sites did not have any protection for the body by a roof of any kind, but the idea of a roof did eventually develop.

By the time of the First and Second Dynasties (c. 3100-2700 B.C.), concepts of after life had become better defined and this is reflected in a greater standardization of burial practices. It was during this period that large brick

The journey to the tomb of Amenemonet, Thebes. The Ramesside Period. A priest leads the way waving an incense-burner.

mastabas (bench-like tomb structures) began to appear containing richly decorated furniture.

In this early period, the Egyptian viewed the human personality as consisting of four basic elements: Knet, the body (or in particular, the dead body); Shut, the shadow; and two elements which were not visible to the scenes--the Ba and the Ka. The earliest heiroglyphic sign for the Ba was the stork. From the Eighteenth Dynasty onward (ca. 1570 B.C.), however, the Ba took the form of a human-headed bird, which was sometimes preceded by a small lighted lamp. In many of the tombs the Ba is depicted as flying around the passages of the tomb or even soaring into upper air. The normal environment was the tomb or its vicinity and it is common to see it hovering over the mummy of the individual.

In the Old Kingdom Period (2700-2200 B.C.), it appears that the Ba was the exclusive possession of the king, but in later times as a "democratization of the hereafter" took place, the term was applied to many individuals.

The term, Ba, is very difficult to define. Some have suggested the word "soul," but this is not adequate since the Ba was an expression of continued function after death or an expression of some aspect of a god's being.[1] It appears that the Ba did not come into existence until after death and only then as a result of special ceremonies designed for this purpose. Henri Frankfort defines the Ba and its function as follows:

> The dead man, conceived as living in animated existence after death, was called Ba. We translate that word, uncomfortably, with "soul," but the Ba was not part of living person, but the whole of a person as he appears after death. The word Ba means "animation, manifestation."[2]

Another term intricately associated with death and the after-life was Ka which every man possessed. The Egyptian view of man's origin was very materially oriented. He

Wooden funerary box which may have originally contained Ushabti figurines. *Courtesy The University Museum, The University of Pennsylvania.*

believed that both his Ka and body were formed on a potter's wheel by the god Khnum. Again, it is difficult to utilize the English word "soul" to translate Ka since the Ka did not reside within the individual's body. According to Egyptian mythology it needed to be nourished and, therefore, appropriate offerings were dedicated to it. The term served to denote man's vital force and sustenance. "With a suitable determinative, the phallus, it designated the bull, and this has been taken as evidence of the creative force."[3]

The word Akh was frequently utilized to describe some metaphysical part of man and had no pictorial form, but when it was written, it appeared as a crested ibis. The term has been variously translated, "beneficial, advantageous or glorious." When applied to a dead man, however, ideas such as "effective being" or "transfigured spirit" would be more appropriate.

The tomb was regarded as the place where transfiguration took place and a man became Akhu ("transfigured spirit") through the funerary ritual. The term occurs as early as the First Dynasty and was common in the tombs of the Old Kingdom. From this it has been concluded that the dead could be manifested on the earth as Ba, but that they were Akhu in their own peculiar and exalted form of existence.[4] This clearly was one of the more important terms used by the ancient Egyptian for the dead.

From mortuary texts, one gets the impression that the Egyptian concept of the after-life was basically an idealized extension of life on earth. Although metaphysical elements of man were recognized, funeral preparations for individuals indicate that the essential functions of the future life were largely physical in nature. For this reason significant quantities of food were often placed in the tombs. This, of course, was not only a common practice in Egypt, but among other ancient cultures as well.

After the individual had experienced a "rebirth" following death, he was believed to have embarked on a dangerous journey which would take him toward the west. For this he needed a boat. Such a voyage included the possibility of attack from demons who were depicted as gigantic snakes or animal-headed monstrosities.

Having successfully crossed the great river in the west, and thwarted the demonic forces, he still faced confrontation with the gods. In order to guarantee success through these perilous aspects of the journey, a series of magical spells was devised. The oldest collection of spells is known as the Pyramid Texts and was discovered on the walls of pyramids dating back to the Fifth and Sixth Dynasties.

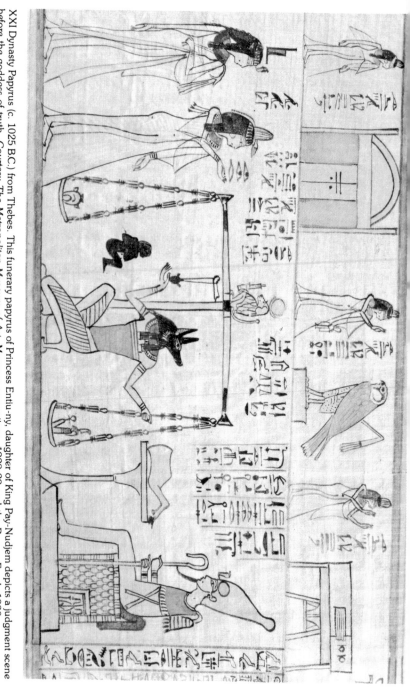

XXI Dynasty Papyrus (c. 1025 B.C.) from Thebes. This funerary papyrus of Princess Entiu-ny, daughter of King Pay-Nudjem depicts a judgment scene before the goddess of truth. *Courtesy The Metropolitan Museum of Art. Museum excavations, 1928-29 and the Rogers Fund, 1930.*

Originally, the magical benefits of the Pyramid Texts were for the royal dead alone, but the Coffin Texts, dating to the Middle Kingdom show that they were later claimed by the commoners as well.

A rather large collection of magical texts written on papyrus is from the New Kingdom. They are known as "The Book of the Dead." More accurately, they should be called the "Books of the Dead" because of their abundance. Large sections of these documents are preoccupied with statements regarding what the individual did not do as a basis for his righteous treatment in judgment. Many of the texts are characterized by self-laudatory expressions indicating good deeds performed during the lifetime of the deceased.

Every individual had to face a tribunal after death. The primary purposes of this court were to prevent the violation of funerary property, weigh human actions in the balance and ultimately determine the fate of every individual. Even great kings had to undergo a trial like this before they could step into the sacred sun-boat and complete their journey.

This judicial process is very vividly illustrated on the famous papyrus of Ani now in the British Museum. Anubis, the jackal-headed god who presided over embalming, is depicted as testing the heart of the scribe, Ani, on the scales. On the right hand side of the scales is the sacred feather symbolizing justice against which the heart was weighed. The Ibis-headed god, Thoth, then records the result. In the light of this, the following plea is significant.

> Heart of my mother, heart of my various forms, rise not up against me as a witness. Oppose me not in the court of justice. Send not the balance down against me before the Guardian of the Scales. For thou art the Ka which is my body, thou art Khnum who strengtheneth my limbs. Mayest thou attain to that good whereto I aspire. Let not my name be in bad odour with the court. Speak no lie against me.[5]

The dead man and his wife embrace their son. From the Stela of Amenemhet discovered in Cairo. Middle Kingdom Period.

If the heart remained silent thus allowing the scales to balance each other perfectly, the declaration was made that the deceased was *maakheru* ("true of voice") and this was duly recorded by Thoth.

The Funerary Ritual

From the Papyrus Ani and many other texts, it is clear that the Egyptian had a well-conceived idea of justice as a requirement for a happy after-life. No Egyptian, including the Pharaoh, was guaranteed a completely blessed eternity apart from the kind of justice portrayed in the Book of the Dead.

Equally vital to the whole process of preparation for life after death was the funerary ritual. Shortly after the death of an individual, the necropolis employees were notified and they proceeded to take the body across the Nile River to the west bank. The weeping family remained at home while the porters carried the body in a sarcophagus to the river. At the river, the corpse was met by eight people including a priest who would accompany it to the purification tent.

Following ceremonial purification rites, the body was dressed in clean clothes and transported on a lion-shaped bier to the embalming tent. The corpse was accompanied by the same officials who had brought the body across the Nile.

A period of seventy days was required for the mummification process. Only the embalmers and priests remained for the preparation of the body which was carried out by well specified procedures. Each aspect of the mummification process was accompanied by a reading from the priest. This, coupled with the period required for the dehydration process, is why so much time elapsed between death and the time of burial.

After mummification had been completed, all the various articles of furniture which had been prepared to accompany the burial were brought to the embalmer's tent where the mummy awaited its final journey. When all had been made ready, the funeral procession left the tent and headed for the tomb.

Leading the procession was the mummy on a sledge pulled by oxen and topped by an open shrine. Friends and relatives would help with the ropes which steadied the sledge while the wife and daughter, or the wife and mother walked at the head and foot of the bier. The number of priests involved in the procession would be in accordance with the importance of the individual. Following the priests were female servants (and friends) who cried out and lamented the death of their master. Professional mourners were often hired who would violently beat their breasts and wail loudly. Dust was poured on the heads as a sign of grief and sorrow, a practice that was also common to the Hebrews.

Following the mourners there were servants carrying food

Muu dancers. Tomb of Autefoqer, Thebes. Early XII Dynasty.

and the furniture which had been prepared as grave goods. The Canopic box holding the four jars which contained the entrails of the deceased was borne on a small sledge.

Another group of individuals who frequently participated in the funeral procession were the Muu dancers. These men were usually waiting at the tomb when the procession arrived and were distinguished by strange crowns of reeds, whose shape resembled the royal white crown of upper Egypt. The dance performed on this occasion probably depicted some aspect of hope for the after-life.

The desire for appropriate ritual was deep-seated in Egyptian religious thought and is eloquently illustrated in the well-known story of Sinuhe. Sinuhe lived during the Middle Kingdom under Amenemhet I and his son, Sesosteris I. Because of certain conditions, Sinuhe left the royal court and his native land. While living in Palestinian exile, a royal decree was issued encouraging Sinuhe to return to the land of the Nile. One of the concerns expressed in this document was that he have a proper Egyptian burial.

> Even to-day thou has begun to be old, thou hast lost thy manhood, and has bethought thee of the day of burial, the passing to honour. An evening is devoted to thee with cedar-oil and with bandages from the hand of Tait. A funeral procession is made for thee on the day of burial; the mummy-shell is of gold, with the head of lapis lazuli; the heaven is above thee, and thou art placed upon a sledge. Oxen drag thee, and singers go before thee, and the dance of the Muu is performed for thee at the door of thy tomb . . . Thus shalt thou not die abroad, nor shall Asiatics bury thee.[6]

When the dance of the Muu was concluded at the tomb, the final, and most important, ceremony that was performed was known as the "opening of the mouth." This rite took place at the Purification Tent until the beginning of the New Kingdom when it was transferred to the entrance of the tomb.

Originally this practice seems to have been associated only with the royal or divine statutes by means of magic, but it was later extended to the corpse itself. The purpose of this ceremony was to restore the vital energy of the dead man thus enabling him to breathe, speak, eat, and drink again. Actually, the officiating priest not only touched the mouth, but the ears also in order to provide for full functions in the future life.

An animal was often sacrificed before the final rites of reanimation were actually started. At the appropriate time, the Sem or Setem priest with his distinctive leopard-skin mantle and shaven head, moved toward the mummy and with the aid of an adze and chisel, opened the mouth and ears. The twenty-first and twenty-second chapters of the

Book of the Dead referred to this ceremony as "giving mouth to the deceased."[7] This whole ceremony was actually performed twice with a few variations the second time.

Following the "opening of the mouth" ceremony, the mummy was then taken into the inner chamber of the tomb where it was laid to rest. Friends and relatives would leave that chamber and make their way up the stairs through the passageway leading to the exit. Other rooms and galleys contained food, drink, and gifts, the quantity and quality of which depended largely on the importance and wealth of the deceased. A poor man would be buried in a shallow grave wrapped in matting or linen, and accompanied by a few jars filled with beer along with some loaves of bread. Pharaohs, on the other hand, were accompanied by the best foods in the land, the survival of which has been of immense importance to archaeologists in reconstructing the diet of the ancient Egyptians.

But what did the Egyptian really believe about the length of time this food would last for the deceased? Surely he did not conclude that the provisions placed in the tomb would last for eternity. Indeed not. In order to care for such long range needs, magical substitutes were utilized. This is vividly portrayed in the beautiful tomb paintings found throughout Egypt. Tables loaded with food and servants bringing additional provisions are common motifs in their funerary art.

In addition to food, fine oil, and perfumes, other precious liquids were placed in the tomb with the body. Other equipment commonly found in the tomb chambers included war implements such as bows, arrows, daggers, shields and swords. Female burials were accompanied by toiletries including tables and small, beautifully decorated boxes.

After all had left the tomb, masons would seal up the mummy chamber. Specially cut stones of limestone and granite were employed for this purpose and the craftsmanship involved in this work was truly remarkable. Stones for

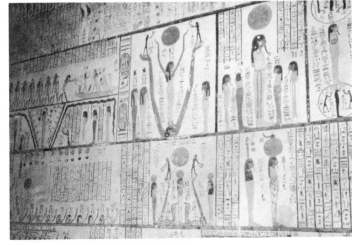

Wall
paintings
from the
royal tombs
at Thebes
(XVIII
Dynasty).
*Photos by
the author.*

such doorways were cut and fitted to a fraction of an inch. In fact, it was quite often impossible to detect the difference between the real doorway to the chamber of the mummy from a number of false doorways which would be made throughout the larger tombs in order to frustrate the attempts at robbery. The entrance of the tomb was carefully conceal- ed, but not usually for a very long time.

Tomb robbing was carried out in ancient Egypt by pro- fessionals, frequently with the knowledge of the royal court. It is, therefore, very rare for one to discover a tomb which had not been rifled in ancient times.

After the funeral rites were complete, the family of the deceased would return to its normal duties with the hope that the preparations were adequate to provide for a safe journey to the west and a peaceful after-life. The comple- tion of the funeral rituals did not mean that the tomb was abandoned, however. Relatives would visit the tombs, not only to make offerings to the Ka, but would gather there on feast days for celebrations, including a meal at which the dead was supposed to be present.

Provisions of proper food for sustaining the Ka in after- life was matter of great concern. In the papyrus of Nu now in the British Museum, there are several chapters which pro- vide spells against the much-dreaded danger of being forced to eat filth in the underworld as a result of the failure of one's relatives to provide sufficient supplies of food and drink.

> The overseer of the palace, Nu, justified, saith: "That which is an abomination to me, that which is an abomination to me, let me not eat. That which is an abomination unto me, that which is abomination to me is filth. Let me not be com- pelled to eat it in the absence of sepulchral cakes and pro- visions which should be offered to me. Let me not be destroyed thereby; let me not be compelled to take it into my hands; and let me not be compelled to walk therein in my sandals."[8]

The failure of relatives and friends to provide proper offerings of food for the deceased was clearly perceived as impacting the quality of after-life. The Egyptian conceived of his situation becoming so desperate as to be forced to eat human waste.

For the wealthy, these fears were probably less in evidence, for their riches would more than provide adequate gifts of food.

It would be incorrect to conclude that the Egyptians possessed a single theology with regard to the after-life. It is clear that there were a number of contradictory ideas concerning death and the future. What we understand to be contradictory, however, was probably not so to the ancient Egyptian. Because of an intricate system of syncretism, he was able to accept conflicting ideas as being mere mysteries, and then work them into one functional system.

3 Tombs, Temples and Pyramids

According to some statistics, about 500 million bodies were mummified in Egypt prior to the Roman period.[1] This massive number of burials, coupled with the abundance of well-prepared mastabas, pyramids, and underground caverns has allowed archaeologists the rare opportunity of studying burial traditions in a way unparalleled elsewhere.

In fact, "the culture of ancient Egypt, more than any other civilization, is symbolized for many people by funerary remains, particularly by bandaged mummies and their painted coffins."[2]

From the abundance of tomb inscriptions and other writings, it is apparent that the wealthy Egyptian was very much occupied with the matter of preparing for death. This was not due to a morbid disposition or irrational abandonment of the value of life here on earth. Rather, it represented a commitment to that which was necessary and appropriate for a life that would be much longer than the one presently enjoyed.

The great Sphinx at Giza. *Photo by the author.*

From the Twenty-second Dynasty (c. 945-745 B.C.) comes the intriguing book entitled, *"The Wisdom of Anii."* The exact origin of this document is shrouded in obscurity, but it contains valuable information of the Egyptian view of practical wisdom. Among the instructions which are given, are special observations concerning the preparation for death.

> Make for thyself a fair abode in the desert-valley, the deep which will hide thy corpse. Have it before thine eyes in thine occupations--even as the great elders, who rest in their sepulchre. He who maketh it (for himself) meeteth with no reproof; good is it if thou art furnished in like manner.[3]

Since death was regarded as a transition from this life to another, rather than the cessation of existence, it is understandable why such careful preparation was necessary for burial. Tombs and funerary equipment were prepared during one's lifetime and mortuary priests were appointed. Thus, when death occurred, one was fully prepared for it and was guaranteed safe passage to the world in the west. Failure to make such preparations would be to risk the possibility of total annihilation from memory, something the Egyptian greatly feared.

For royalty, death meant the transition from this life to a kingly position on the throne of Osiris. Mortuary texts found inside of the pyramids of Unis (Fifth Dynasty) and Pepi II (Sixth Dynasty) reflect the Egyptian attitude toward the death of their king.

> O King Unis, thou has not at all departed dead, thou has departed living! For thou sittest upon the throne of Osiris, with thy scepter in thy hand, that thou mightest give command to the living, and with the grip of thy wand in thy hand, that thou mightest give command to those secret of place . . .
>
> O Atum, the one here is that son of thine, Osiris, whom thou has caused to survive and to live on. He lives--(so also) this king Unis lives. He does not die--(so also) this king Unis does not die. He does not perish--(so also) this king Unis does not perish.[4]

Colossal Statues of Pharaoh Amenhotep III in Western Thebes. *Photo by the author.*

While the idea of continued life and identity was firmly established in the mind of the Egyptians, there were still lingering fears and doubts regarding the transition to that life. Deep concerns existed regarding the safety of the mummy and the security of the tomb. After all, the tomb was his dwelling place and if his immortal spirit was to survive, the body had to survive as well.

> So, while they admitted that man suffered physical death and nevertheless survived, they could not imagine such a survival without a physical substratum. Man without a body seemed incomplete and ineffectual. He required his body in perpetuity, as if it were the concrete basis of his individuality.[5]

In the light of this sentiment, it is easy to understand why the intricate process of mummification was developed and why such care was taken to protect the tomb from the ubiquitous robber.

As observed in the previous chapter, a statue with a man's name on it was originally the object of the "opening of the mouth" ceremony. By granting magical animation to this statue, the deceased was guaranteed a functioning body, even if the original one decayed or was destroyed.[6]

Tragic, indeed, was the thirst of the tomb robber for the ornaments, gold and other valuables in the chambers of the dead. For this reason, so-called curses were included in the tomb's funerary inscriptions in order to discourage violation of the tomb and its occupants. These curses normally threatened the thief with after-life judgment or with other-world vengeance by the deceased who dwelt with the gods.

The following text comes from the tomb of a Sixth Dynasty magistrate, Nenki of Sakkara, and illustrates well the nature of these tomb curses.

> As for this tomb, which I have made in the Necropolis of the West, I made it (in) a clean and central place. As for any noble, any official, or any man who shall rip out any stone or any brick from this tomb, I will be judged with him by the Great God, I (will) seize his neck like a bird, and I will cause all the living who are upon the earth to be afraid of the spirits who are in the West, which is (still) far from them.[7]

Protecting the tomb from disturbance was a matter of utmost importance since the security of the future life was at stake. The Egyptian association between the mummy and magical power is seen in the fact that most tomb robbers mutilated the mummies before leaving the tomb. Was this their way of eliminating the curse upon them? Apparently so.

The Tomb Robbers

It is ironic that the most sacred thing in Egyptian culture, the burial with its gifts for the after-life, was treated with such a blasphemous activity as tomb robbery.

The desecration of tombs in ancient Egypt was a well organized and profitable activity. As in modern tomb robbery, local officials were frequently involved in the process either directly or indirectly. The motive behind such ghoulish activity is well described by Fred Bratton, "As it was, human greed was stronger than human piety and the repose of the kings, who had taken such precaution to make sure of their happiness in the realms of Osiris, was rudely disturbed by cunning and skillful robbers."[8]

Indications are that this activity reached its peak during the Twentieth Dynasty when Theban priests betrayed the trust given to them, and opted rather for the easy wealth which came their way as gifts from the robbers.

With the discovery of the Abbott Papyrus, startling evidence has surfaced regarding the nature and extent of these robberies. According to these documents, a quarrel broke out between the mayor of Thebes, the "City of the Living" on the east bank of the Nile, and his counterpart, the mayor of the "City of the Dead" on the west bank. Paser, mayor of east Thebes during the reign of Ramses IX (ca. 1120 B.C.), accused Paweraa, mayor and guardian of the necropolis west of the Nile, of negligence and possible complicity in a series of royal tomb robberies.

A vizier appointed a commission to investigate and he put the mayor of the necropolis in charge of the investiga-

An uncoffined "mummy" of the Second Dynasty. From *Archaic Egypt* by W. B. Emery. *Courtesy Penguin Books Ltd.*

A subsidiary burial of the early First Dynasty. From *Archaic Egypt* by W. B. Emery. *Courtesy Penguin Books Ltd.*

Subsidiary burial of the early First Dynasty, containing the skeleton of a dwarf. From *Archaic Egypt* by W. B. Emery. *Courtesy Penguin Books Ltd.*

tion! Such a suspicious appointment might lead one to wonder about the innocence of the vizier in matters involving the dead. The investigating team did find some tombs rifled, but a further inquiry the next day at the temple of Amun saw Paser lose his battle. Paweraa denied the charges, and the vizier accepted his testimony. Paser was not heard from again, and tomb robberies continued while Paweraa remained in office unscathed.

Later, however, some thieves did confess their crimes, and the description of their activities is of special interest because it provides information on the situation of the original burial and the objects placed with it.

> King's wife, Nubkhas (life! health! strength!) his royal wife in the place of his sepulchre, it being protected with mortar covered with blocks. We penetrated them all, we found her resting likewise. We opened their coffins and the coverings in which they were. We found the august mummy of this king . . . There was a numerous list of amulets and gold ornaments at its throat; its head had a mask of gold upon it; the august mummy of this king was overlaid with gold throughout. Its coverings were wrought with gold and silver, within and without, inlaid with every splendid costly stone. We stripped off the gold which we found on the august mummy of this god, and its amulets and ornaments which were at its throat, the coverings wherein it rested. We found the king's wife likewise; we stripped off all that we found on her likewise. We set fire to their coverings. We stole their furniture, which we found with them, being vases of gold, silver and bronze. We divided, and made the gold which we found on these two gods, on their mummies and the amulets, and coverings, into eight parts.[9]

The operation of the thieves around the necropolis was indeed disastrous. They exhibited little regard for either the beauty or sanctity of the burials, and when their clandestine activity was finished, the tomb was left in a shambles. Papyrus Amherst provides this graphic description of the situation.

> It was found that the thieves had broken into them all, that

they had pulled out their occupants from their coverings, and had thrown them upon the ground; and that they had stolen their articles of house furniture which had been given to them, together with gold, the silver, and the ornaments which were in their coverings.[10]

As a result of systematic plundering in antiquity, no royal tomb has ever been discovered completely untouched by thieves, including the tomb of Tutankhamen. The chambers of this now famous Eighteenth Dynasty king had been entered and were in the process of being plundered when the thieves were either caught or scared off. Evidence of a hasty exit from the tomb exists in a small handkerchief filled with rings that had been collected then dropped by the robbers.

It is not only profitable to study the mummies and their associated burial equipment, but it is equally vital to examine the development of burial practices and tomb construction in ancient Egypt.

The Early Years (4500-2700 B.C.)

In the pre-Dynastic period, the Egyptian was buried in a shallow grave in the desert sands and usually surrounded with pottery jars containing food. The contracted or fetal position was generally adopted for burial in this period with the body wrapped in either matting or animal skins. Somewhat later, the dead were placed in very crudely made baskets, boxes or pottery coffins which were, in turn, buried in the sand or deposited in natural caves along the Nile Valley.

During the first two Dynasties the tombs consisted of large rectangles built of unbaked brick and adorned on the outside with projections and niches. The coffin consisted of a simple wooden chest, which was placed in an underground vault along with furniture and pottery. Considerable amounts of food and drink, along with earthen vessels, weapons, pottery and even games have been found with such burials.

he body of this elderly adult was probably
aced in some form of wicker basket and
overed with animal skin. Some patches of
en are also present on the body surface. Late
redynastic Period. *Courtesy the British
useum.*

Body of a male adult lying in a flexed position
from the Late Predynastic Period. *Courtesy the
British Museum.*

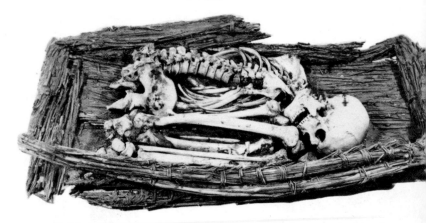

Skeleton of an adult, sex uncertain, lying in a flexed position on the left side in a cane basket. Predynastic Period — First Dynasty. *Courtesy the British Museum.*

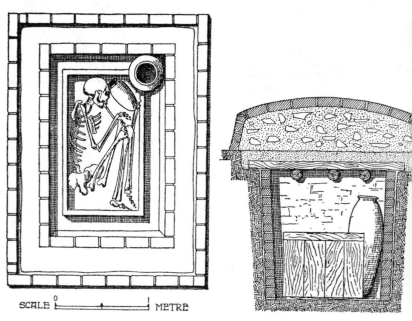

SCALE 0 METRE

Tomb of the artisan and servant class of the early First Dynasty. From *Archaic Egypt* by W. B. Emery. *Courtesy Penguin Books Ltd.*

Of course, for the poor Egyptian the shallow desert grave was still in vogue. From this time onward, the Egyptian tomb began to follow a certain pattern which consisted of two essential parts; the burial chamber and a room in which the offerings for the dead were placed. The tombs of most kings and important nobles consisted of a shallow pit, cut not more than eight to ten feet below ground level. In this pit a series

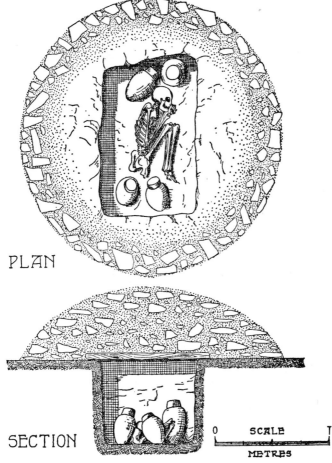

PLAN

SECTION

Tomb of the poor class of the early First Dynasty. From *Archaic Egypt* by W. B. Emery. *Courtesy Penguin Books Ltd.*

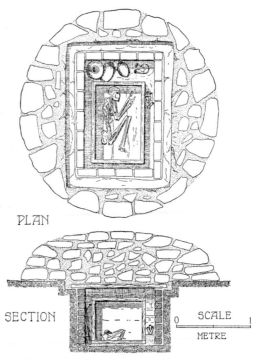

PLAN

SECTION

SCALE

0

METRE

Poor-class burial of the middle First Dynasty. From *Archaic Egypt* by W. B. Emery. *Courtesy Penguin Books Ltd.*

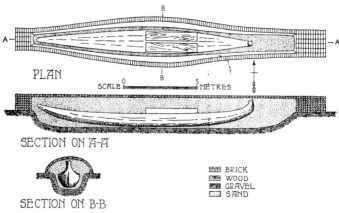

PLAN

SCALE 0 — 5 METRES

SECTION ON A-A

SECTION ON B-B

▦	BRICK
▧	WOOD
▨	GRAVEL
▢	SAND

Reconstruction of a boat burial. From *Archaic Egypt* by W. B. Emery. *Courtesy Penguin Books Ltd.*

of brick-built rooms was erected, the central and largest being reserved for the burial and the remainder to accomodate all the precious objects of the funerary equipment.

The sub-structure was roofed with timber beams and planks, and the mouth of the pit above it was usually filled with rubble. Above this substructure, on ground level, was erected the so-called "mastaba" (an Arabic word meaning "bench"). This consisted of a rectangular mask of brick work with an elaborate panelled exterior. The greater axis of the rectangle was, without exception, oriented from north to south. This type of tomb continued through the Second Dynasty.

The Old Kingdom (2700-2200 B.C.)

A revolution in funerary architecture took place at the beginning of the Third Dynasty as stone took the place of brick in monumental structures. The architectural concept of the mastaba was altered and expanded, ultimately becom-

Three Mastabas at Giza. From *The Mummy* by E. A. Wallis Budge. *Courtesy Cambridge University Press.*

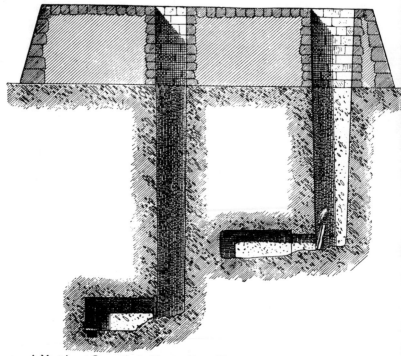

A Mastaba at Giza with double pits. From *The Mummy* by E. A. Wallis Budge. *Courtesy Cambridge University Press.*

ing a pyramid. As one travels along the plateau of the Lybian desert to the west and the northwest of the village of Sakkara, he encounters a most amazing sight. Rising out of the desert sands is the famous Step-Pyramid of King Zoser, one of the most important monarchs of the Third Dynasty.

The pyramid constructed by him is one of the oldest hitherto discovered and represents one of the earliest monumental stone structures in Egypt. His chief minister and designer of the tomb was the well-known Imhotep, who was something of a Michelangelo, a genius skilled in several fields including medicine and architecture. After his death, he was deified and still later the Greeks equated him with the patron-god of medicine, Aesculapius.

This magnificent structure covers more than 37 acres. The enclosure walls are 34½ feet high, 1795 feet long from north to south, and 914 feet from west to east, the total length all around being more than a mile!

The Step-Pyramid was actually developed from a mastaba and heightened to six "steps," or stages, until the total height was 204 feet. The separate steps, each set back six and one-half feet from that below it, vary from 28 feet to 37½ feet in height. The pyramid itself was built of limestone and in many places is in a crumbled condition today. The king's burial chamber was constructed of granite at the bottom of a wide shaft nearly 100 feet deep. An opening was left in the ceiling to allow the mummy to be inserted, and was afterwards blocked by a granite plug.

Smaller shafts led to more vaults which were intended for the queen and the princess. As in the case of the old brick mastabas, this tomb had many (14) false doors which were intended to frustrate robbery efforts. Only a single real door gave access to the interior.

The Step-Pyramid of Zoser, one of the important kings of the III Dynasty. *Photo by the author.*

From this time onward, the development of the standard pyramid was inevitable. Imhotep had established a practical standard for the great rulers of the Old Kingdom who reigned as gods and hence, were the state. This period was one of the greatest epochs in Egypt's long history and was characterized by centralized absolutism. The king ruled with unchallengable power and dominance. In part, the great power and sacred prestige of the god-king were symbolized in the massive pyramids constructed to be his final resting place.

Why were these monumental burial sites always located on the west side of the Nile valley? There are two primary reasons: first, the Egyptians believed the realm of the dead lay in the west, and second, the location had to have a solid rock base in order to support the weight of such massive monuments as the pyramids.

One cannot help but be struck with awe as he approaches the three great Old Kingdom pyramids at Giza. The first and the most impressive of these is the Great Pyramid, built by Khufu (Cheops) with an original height of 481 feet. It is so massive that the volume of it would allow St. Peter's in Rome, St. Paul's in London, Westminster Abbey, and the cathedrals of Florence and Milan to be put inside, were it not solid. Its present height is approximately 450 feet. The sloping sides of this pyramid were originally about 614 feet, although today they are only 571 feet.

About 2,300,000 blocks, weighing an average of two and one-half tons apiece, were used in its construction. In all, about six and one-quarter million tons of stone were employed. But it is not the mere mass of this great pyramid that staggers the imagination, but the marvelous technology and craftsmanship which is exhibited in the tightly-fitted joints. Wilson describes this commitment to precision as follows:

> Here were six and a quarter million tons of stone, with casing blocks averaging as much as two and half tons each.

A view of the Great Pyramid at Giza from the bottom of the North-west corner.
(Arrow indicates man standing near base.) *Photo by the author.*

Yet those casing blocks were dressed and fitted with a joint of 1/50 of an inch—a scrupulous nicety worthy of the jeweler's craft. Here the margin of error in the squareness of the north and south sides, was 0.09 percent, and of the east and west sides, 0.03 percent. This mighty mass of stone was set upon a dressed rock pavement which, from the opposite corners, had a deviation from a true plane of only 0.004 percent.[11]

The second pyramid at Giza which originally stood 471 feet high (although today only measures 447 ½ feet), was constructed by Khafre (Chefren). Connected with the pyramid complex is a funerary temple in which huge limestone blocks were used for construction. This structure is commonly called the Valley Chapel. East of this pyramid is the famous Sphinx, the height of which, from the top of the head to the ground, is 66 feet. The length from the paws to the tail is 240 feet.

Menkaure's (Mycenrinus) pyramid at Giza stands only 204 feet today with sides measuring 365½ feet and the slopes, 252½ feet. There is a mortuary temple on either side of the structure.

The decreased size of this pyramid and subsequent ones may have political and economic implications. It is well-known that the absolute power of the king went into decline after the Fourth Dynasty. This, coupled with the exorbitant cost of building elaborate non-economic structures, required a more modest approach to the establishment of mortuary sites.

The question often arises as to the precise function of these massive pyramids. At the risk of receiving additional mail from irate numerologists and pyramidologists, allow me to again affirm that the sole function of these pyramids was as a burial site for the king and his family. Their massive size was intended to be a reflection of the king's great power and, further, to provide maximum security for the mummified body of the king. Much ado has been made of these

The large pyramids at Giza built by Menkaure, Khafre and Khufu of the III Dynasty. *Photo by the author.*

structures by creative pyramidologists who contend that the "mysterious number combinations" and "sacred symmetry" have prophetic value.[12]

Equally fanciful are those suggestions which maintain that these burial sites were constructed by men from outer space. This view has emerged on the premise that the whole appearance of these monuments is an unexplainable mystery. Only those buried in literary obscurantism could reach such conclusions. With the abundance of scholarly material on the methods and materials utilized in the construction of the pyramids at Giza as well as the others in Egypt, more reasonable and rational conclusions are required.

The actual techniques employed in the building of these monuments are now well known due to the intensive studies done on the massive structures during the past century. The pyramid of Khufu has probably been analyzed, measured, studied and described more than any other monument in Egypt.

According to historian Herodotus, the construction of the pyramid took 20 years to complete. The king, he reports, employed 100,000 men for periods of three months to transport the stone. Most Egyptologists believe this number is too large. Petrie, for example, suggested that 100,000 may have been employed in a given year while others have argued that no more than 2,500 men could have worked on the actual face of the pyramid at a single time.

Kurt Mendelssohn suggests that "assuming, as seems not unreasonable, that the time needed for one crew to bring building material from the quarry to the pyramid and putting it into place varied between one to three days, we end up with a work force of about 50,000 men."[13]

Preparations for the actual construction of the pyramid began by first leveling the plateau area. This was done by removing the sand and gravel down to bedrock. The area to be leveled was surrounded with low walls of brick and then flooded. By measuring down from a number of points from the surface of the water, a network of trenches of equal depth could be cut. When the water was released, the areas would then be leveled down to the bottom of the trenches.

This method of leveling would have come naturally to the Egyptians since they had hundreds of years of experience with flooded fields and irrigation trenches much like these. In the case of the Great Pyramid, the platform was not completely leveled so the core could be built into the structure. That this method of leveling was employed is confirmed by the fact that the prevailing winds from north of the Cairo area caused precisely the error from true level on water surfaces that is actually found on the plateau of the Great Pyramid. The pyramid was constructed in such a way that its four sides faced the four cardinal points, yet another indicator of the technical genius of the builders and architects.

The majority of the material used in the pyramid was limestone which was cut in nearby quarries both on the east and west sides of the Nile, then brought to the site on sleds. The casing stones placed over the surface of the pyramid, giving a beautiful white appearance, probably came from the Tura quarries just across the river from Giza. The quarried stone was cut and prepared using copper or bronze tools,

A procession carrying the funerary furniture of Ramose. From the tomb of Ramose, Thebes. Reign of Amenhotep III.

although hard stone tools may have been employed as well.

How, then, were these massive stones moved into place? There is general agreement that massive sloping ramps of brick and earth were utilized which were removed when the pyramid was completed. For maneuvering the large blocks, they used ropes, sledges, levers and cradles. Gypsum was employed as a lubricating medium to enable the masons to slide the blocks into place.

The great care taken in the preparation of this pyramid reflects the intense desire on the part of the King and his subjects to make adequate preparation for his burial. Some have even suggested that these massive pyramids were under construction as a matter of state policy, even before a king took the throne.[14]

In this early period immortality was the possession of the king alone so if he survived, there would be hope for those associated with him. Burials of the nobles tended to be clustered around the pyramids or in the vicinity. Provincial cemetaries were rare in the Fourth Dynasty, but by the Sixth Dynasty, they were the rule. It was during the Sixth Dynasty that the power of the king began to decline leading to greater individualism among the nobles. No longer were the burials of nobility clustered around that of the king. Burial traditions of the queens began to change, prerogatives that were exclusively those of the kings were ascribed to the queens and the worship of Re enjoyed a resurgence.

In spite of careful preparations and security measures, all the tombs of these early kings were robbed not long after their burials. The technology and layout of the great pyramids were not well-kept secrets, and in all likelihood, some of the robberies were carried out with knowledge of court officials. A recorded lament from the First Intermediate Period indicates that many of the tombs had been desecrated by the end of the Sixth Dynasty.

> Behold now, something has been done which never happened for a long time; the king has been taken away by poor men. Behold, he who was buried as a (divine) falcon is (now) on a (mere) bier; what the pyramid hid has become empty.[15]

In the light of the Egyptian's concept of the after-life, one can appreciate the despair reflected in these texts, for with the mutilation of the mummy comes the serious question of his divine survival.

Tombs of the Middle and New Kingdoms (2050-1070 B.C.)

The early kings of the Twelfth Dynasty, who resided at Ithttoui, built pyramids somewhat like those of the Old Kingdom at Dahsur, Lisht, and the entrance to the Fayuum. They rise to about 200 feet and are generally in a poor state of preservation today. Some of these pyramids were con-

The sarcophagus of Amenhotep II of the XVIII Dynasty. *Photo by the author.*

Mummy of Amenhotep II in the royal tomb in Thebes. *Courtesy the Matson Photo Service.*

The funerary temple of Queen Hatshepsut at Deir el-Bahri (XVIII Dynasty). *Photo by the author.*

structed of brick. It was during this period that a shift away from mastabas and pyramids to the rock-cut tombs took place. The first Theban Pharaohs hollowed out caverns such as Dreh Abul Nega in the northern sector of the Necropolis. From the time of Thutmoses I onward, most of them prepared burial places in the valleys which lay behind the last spur of the Lybian mountains to the west of the Nile River.

The tombs of this period have three characteristic parts: the chapel, the passage to the sarcophagus chamber, and the sarcophagus chamber itself, excavated in solid rock. Sometimes, however, the chapel or chamber in which the relatives of the deceased assembled from time to time was above the ground and separate from the tomb, as it was in the days of the great pyramids.

Mummies of the Middle Kingdom were often placed on

their side in a rectangular wooden coffin on which were painted the mortuary texts often designated "Coffin Texts." These inscriptions were actually excerpts from the older Pyramid Texts, with some variations. By the time of the Eighteenth Dynasty, the mummiform type of coffin had come into general use. The Pyramid Texts and Coffin Texts had now been expanded into what has come to be known as "The Book of the Dead." Papyrus rolls containing the Book of the Dead were frequently placed in the tomb with the mummy and sections were sometimes employed to decorate the coffin.

The tombs of the Eighteenth Dynasty kings were some of the most spectacular in all of Egypt. Buried in the Necropolis of Thebes on the west bank of the Nile, the kings spared no expense in chamber preparations. Magnificently painted walls depicting traditional religious motifs and important events associated with the king are an impressive display of technical precision.

The City of the Dead is comprised of the following: the tombs of the kings; the Valley of the Kings (Biban el Muluk) in the extreme west; and the Valley of the Queens (Biban el Hareem) in the extreme south of the Necropolis; tombs of the nobles on the edge of the desert; and mortuary temples of the kings between the mountains and the valley.

Unlike the practices of the kings of the Old Kingdom who built pyramidal structures for burial, Pharaohs of the New Kingdom cut their tombs deep into the living rock. These tombs generally follow the same plan: three corridors, one after the other, leading to the burial chamber itself. At the side of the first corridor are small side chambers, and at the sides of the second and third corridors, rooms for the funerary equipment. The walls and pillars of the tombs are usually decorated with inscriptions and religious scenes. Sixty-four tombs are known to exist in the Valley of the Kings, but most of them are either in ruins or are inaccessible. There

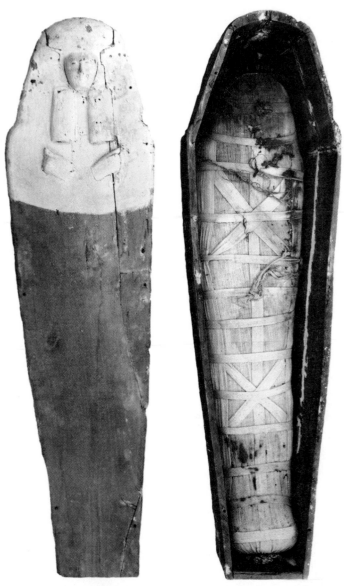

Anthropoid coffin with mummy from a XX Dynasty tomb at Meydum. *Courtesy The University Museum, The University of Pennsylvania.*

are seventeen that are easily accessible, and one, the tomb of Seti I, is a must for any visitor to the area.

The main corridor is 330 feet long and is beautifully preserved. Dating from the Nineteenth Dynasty, the walls are lavishly decorated with some of the most exquisite paintings to be found anywhere. Unfortunately, this tomb, like the others in the area, was pillaged by robbers in antiquity. The tomb was discovered in 1817 by the Italian explorer, Belzoni and the mummy was preserved in a cave at Deir el-Bahri. The mummy now resides in the Cairo Museum and is considered one of the best preserved of all the royal mummies.

For the poor, such tombs, of course, were not available. A cave in the mountains provided the sepulchre for most. The numerous rock caves in the mountains west of Thebes contain masses of decayed mummies and bones several feet deep. Sometimes pits were dug as common graves for a whole town and often the pit or the passage of a forsaken tomb served to accommodate hundreds of bodies. The funerary assemblages of the poor consisted of little more than what they wore day by day. Protective amulets, figures of the gods, scarabs and some pottery adorned the final resting place of these humble folks.

The extremely poor citizen of the New Kingdom was normally given a perfunctory ceremonial cleansing, covered with a cloth, then buried in the sand. The real ambition of every Egyptian, of course, was to have a well-mummified body and a tomb with perpetual care. For the wealthy this was in reach, but the poor had to utilize primitive symbolic emblems with the burial in order to give some magical assurances for a good after-life.

Graeco-Roman Tombs (330 B.C. - A.D. 100)

Under the Ptolemies and the Roman emperors the arrangement of the tombs in Egypt varied significantly. The outer chapel, or chamber, disappeared entirely and the character of everything pertaining to the service of the tomb changed. This, of course, was to be expected in the light of the different religious concepts brought to Egypt by the Greeks and Romans. Tombs became much smaller and lacked the elaborate decorations which were so characteristic of the earlier burials.

Exploration for unopened tombs continues in Egypt with the hope that the archaeologists will get there before the robbers. Being able to examine complete funerary assemblages and unmarred mummies provides enormous amounts of information impacting our historical and cultural understanding of the ancient Egyptian. The extremely dry climate of land west of the Nile makes the survival of rare organic materials a real possibility, but only through the cooperative efforts of many nations can these be discovered and properly studied.

4 Embalmers and Mummies

The dark, dusty chambers of Egypt's many tombs continue to yield fascinating remnants of the past, the most important of which is the actual mummified body. A strong commitment to well-defined burial rites, meticulous care in tomb construction, and patient preparation of the actual body by the ancient Egyptian have provided the archaeologist with an endless array of artifacts with which to study the land of the Nile.

Modern man generally views death as the end of earthly activity followed by the rapid decay of the body's elements. Thus, when confronted with the well-preserved remains of a king who lived more than 3000 years ago, he is awe-struck. The realities of ancient Egyptian history never really impact an individual very dramatically until he comes face to face with the mummified remains of the great Ramses II or Amenhotep III in the Cairo Museum.

Someone has defined a mummy as "a person pressed for time," but the term more seriously is applied to any

Pharaoh Amenhotep III of the Eighteenth Dynasty.

human, animal, bird, fish or reptile that has been preserved by artificial means. The word "mummy," strangely enough, is not actually of Egyptian or Coptic origin. The term is apparently derived from the Byzantine Greek word *moumia* (or *momion*) which has its origins in an Arabic word meaning "a bitumenized thing" or "a body preserved by bitumen." While the latter notion is clearly incorrect in connection with the physical treatment of the ancient Egyptian's body, it does provide an etymological origin for the term. The Egyptian hieroglyphic word for mummy is *sahu*, and the term employed to indicate the act of making a dead man into a mummy is *ges*, meaning to "wrap up in bandages."[1]

The present question, however, is exactly how these bodies were mummified by the ancient embalmer. Due to

Pharaoh Seti I of the Nineteenth Dynasty.

the careful study of ancient inscriptions, combined with modern chemical analysis of the bodies, we now know the basic processes followed by the mummy makers.

The Origin of Mummification

The exact time and place of the origin of mummification is not known. In all likelihood, the idea for artificially preparing the human body for survival was conceived from the accidental discovery of preserved bodies in the desert sands. In pre-Dynastic times the dead were buried in shallow, dry, sandy graves without coffins or wrappings. It is possible that these bodies, with skin and bones intact, were exposed by shifting sands, or dug up by wild dogs. In addition, many burials may have been found accidently by construction activity.

These remarkable pre-Dynastic burials survived because the intense heat of the sand very quickly dehydrated the flesh, leaving it with the appearance of dried leather. The life-like appearance of these corpses certainly would have

A peasant bringing pelicans from the tomb of the royal scribe, Horemheb at Thebes. Reign of Thutmoses IV.

The Tollund man, preserved in a peat bog in Denmark for 2000 years. An excellent example of accidental preservation. *Courtesy Cornell University Press.*

The Tollund man completely uncovered. The body was discovered in a peat bog in 1950. Other bodies have been preserved in like manner in other parts of Denmark. Note the rope around the neck attesting the manner of death. *Courtesy Cornell University Press.*

impressed early Dynastic inhabitants causing them to consider further steps in the preservation of the dead. Having already concluded that man's "spirit" lives on, it became important to provide a physical body to meet the needs of such continued existence. Maintaining the life-like appearance not only guaranteed the identity of that individual in the next world, but allowed his Ba to return to the correct body.

Accidental preservation of the flesh of human and animal remains was not limited to Egypt, but has been observed in the ice deposits of Antarctica and the peat bogs of western Europe. One of the most spectacular discoveries of the latter type was made in 1837 when a well-preserved woman's body was uncovered in a peat bog in Haraldskjaer, Denmark. In more recent times several Iron Age men have been recovered from the bogs at Tollund and Grauballe in central Jutland.

The Tollund man, who died about 2000 years ago, was discovered on a spring day, May 8, 1950. Since that time extensive studies have been pursued on this man as well as others like him. The preservation of the Tollund man with the rope still around his neck indicating the manner of his death, is really quite remarkable.[2]

Equally impressive to the curious visitor are the famous mummies of the catacombs of Guanajuato, Mexico. To see these preserved bodies, many of which still have clothing on, one must go to the town's cemetery and enter the catacombs from above. Once you are past the piles of bones of those who had fought for Father Morelos, a short journey down a passageway leads you to an opening in which you find yourself face to face with the mummified remains of people who had died anywhere from five to 100 years ago.

The reason for their presence as explained by the caretaker is that relatives were not able to pay the twenty pesos a year for a cemetery plot. The bodies in the catacombs are mostly those of relatives who were delinquent in their cemetery payment. There is a provision by which a villager can pay 170 pesos and be guaranteed permanent interment, but very few are able to raise that much money at one time. As a result of this tradition, dozens of bodies line the walls of the catacombs staring into space with eyeless sockets. Skin and clothing are intact, and a few even have handwritten signs around their neck. It is the extremely dry condition of the sand that dehydrated these bodies and provided for their preservation.[3]

The earliest experiments in Egyptian mummification were probably made in the First Dynasty upon royal personages when spacious chamber tombs came into use. A 35-year old woman who lived during the Second Dynasty was found in a wooden coffin at Sakkara by J.E. Quibell. The mummy was resting on its left side and was completely wrapped in a complex series of linen bandages. More than sixteen layers were still intact on the surface, and at least as many more underneath were destroyed. Each limb of the body was bandaged separately. These meager attempts at mummification represent some of the earliest stages in the development of what would become an important profession. During the Second and Third Dynasties, it is assumed

The preparation of this mummy has been carried out with great care and skill by the embalmer. This adult man is dated to the Roman Period. The features of the face are painted upon the outermost wrappings — a reversion to the custom of the Pyramid Age. Note that the fingers and toes are each wrapped separately. *Courtesy the British Museum.*

that this process was continued and improved.

By the time of the Pyramid Age (Fourth and Fifth Dynasties), mummification was undergoing a series of changes. As early as the Fourth Dynasty the embalmers opened the body by an incision in the left flank through which the vicera were removed and placed in Canopic jars. A well-preserved mummy of a man from the Fifth Dynasty rested in the Museum of the Royal College of Surgeons in London until it suffered destruction as the result of World War II activities.

When originally discovered, this mummy was lying on its left side in a fully extended position. The vicera had been removed through an incision in the left flank, and the body cavity was packed with a mass of linen impregnated with resin which had set and dried to a stony hardness. The body and limbs were wrapped with a considerable quantity of very fine linen which had been dipped in resin and then made to fit the contours of the body before hardening. During these early stages of development, mummification procedures did not call for the removal of the brain as was the case later. It would appear, therefore, that current evidence points to the Fourth Dynasty as the beginning of the type of mummification that resulted in the preservation of flesh as well as bones. Prior to the Fourth Dynasty, most of the bodies survived as a jumble of bones inside a hollow shell of resin-soaked bandages.

Mummification was apparently not widely practiced during the turbulent First Intermediate Period. Bodies which have been recovered are simply wrapped with linen.

During the Middle Kingdom period the techniques of mummification went through drastic modifications, and in many respects, significant improvements. The practice of modeling the surface of the body in plaster or resin-soaked linen had been generally abandoned. It was now treated with resin or gum and linen was employed to fill the abdominal

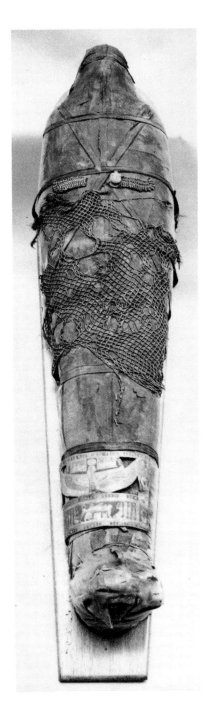

Above: The mummy of a man aged between 23-30 from the XXI Dynasty. According to radiographic studies the mouth is closed and artificial eyes were inserted in the orbits. At right: An adult woman dating from the XXI Dynasty. *Courtesy the British Museum.*

cavity. The brain, however, was still not removed during this time.

The discovery of Eleventh Dynasty mummies at Deir el-Bahri by the Metropolitan Museum during the 1920's gave further evidence of change in mummification patterns, at least in that region.[4] A group of mummified princesses had been dehydrated with the use of dry natron, a technique that would become standard during the New Kingdom. Their flesh was then coated with resin after which they were wrapped. It is worthy of note that these bodies were not eviscerated, but the entrails were removed and ". . . it seems from the dilated rectum and vagina that an oleo-resin (akin to turpentine) was injected into the anus in order to dissolve the organs for removal."[5]

Rock-cut tombs which had come into use during the First Intermediate Period, were now the rule during the Middle Kingdom Period. Decorated chapels and burial chambers became more ornate, and special attention was given to those magical scenes that would assure good provision in the after-life. Painted religious texts are found on most of the coffins along with excerpts from the Old Pyramid Texts.

The classic period of mummification was clearly the New Kingdom era when the mummification type of coffin came into general use. If the individual being buried was wealthy or of high rank, his corpse would be placed in a series of coffins, each fitting inside the other with the inner one the most ornate. Quite often the outer coffin would be carved from limestone in mummy form or would consist of a huge stone sarcophagus. The "Coffin Texts" found on the decorated coffins of the Middle Kingdom Period formed the basis of the New Kingdom Book of the Dead. This collection of prayers was commonly written on papyrus and placed with the body in the coffin.

During the Twenty-first Dynasty (1090-945 B.C.), the custom of using artificial eyes became quite prevalent. The

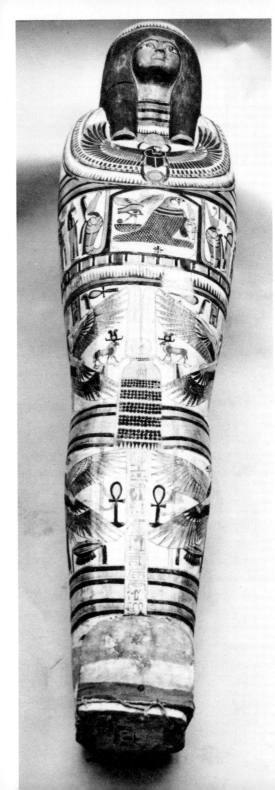

A priest, aged 30-40 years, named Nesperennub, son of Ankhefenkhons of the XXI Dynasty. *Courtesy the British Museum.*

motive for doing this, of course, was to maintain a life-like appearance. It was also for this reason that they packed the body and limbs with sawdust and other materials. During this time the body was sometimes painted all over with ochre—red in the case of men and yellow for women. These special techniques employed during the Twenty-first Dynasty were maintained throughout the Twenty-second (945-745 B.C.) and Twenty-third (745-718 B.C.) Dynasties.

Following the Twenty-third Dynasty the work of the embalmer began to deteriorate as less attention was paid to the details of the treatment of the body, and more to the external appearance of the coffin. From the Twenty-sixth Dynasty (663 B.C.) onward, the custom of restoring the viscera to the body was usually given up, and they were either packed and placed between their legs or deposited in Canopic jars, the use of which was revived and continued until the Ptolemaic period.

During the Graeco-Roman periods, mummification was extended to virtually all segments of society, but with considerably less skill than was exhibited in the empire periods. Communal tombs were employed where mummified bodies could be efficiently stacked. Unfortunately, many of these were destroyed in the process of storage. Small wooden tags were utilized to identify the various bodies as they were buried. Mummification practices faded during the Byzantine period as Christians opted for simple shroud burials.

The fifth century B.C. Greek historian, Herodotus has provided valuable information on mummification, and while most will not agree with some of the details of his account, he does appear to have been party to reliable information. Much of what Herodotus wrote in the fifth century was confirmed by Diodorus Siculus who visited Egypt 400 years later. Herodotus maintained that there were three kinds of embalming, depending on the wealth and importance of the family of the deceased. The first and most expensive method was the one in which great care was taken in maintaining all the rituals and procedures in the mummification process. The second kind eliminated removal of the viscera by hand and utilized oleo-resins to dissolve the entrails instead. The third method, according to Herodotus, only involved clearing the abdomen and then dehydrating the body in preparation for burial.

The Methods of Mummification

One cannot actually speak of only one method of mummification in ancient Egypt, for there were many during its long history. Some of the basic procedures were maintained through time, but a number of variations were introduced for either religious, economic, practical or political purposes. Herodotus described the process as follows:

First they draw out the brains through the nostrils with an iron hook, taking part of it out in this manner, the rest by

Removal of the viscera as depicted in a tomb in Alexandria. Note that the principal gods of the cemetary are represented. *Photo by the author.*

the infusion of drugs. Then with a sharp Ethiopian stone they make an incision in the side, and take out all the bowels; and having cleansed the abdomen and rinsed it with palm wine, they next sprinkle it with pounded perfumes. Then having filled the belly with pure myrrh pounded and cassia, and other perfumes, frankincense excepted, they sew it up again; and when they have done this, they steep it in natron, leaving it under for seventy days; for a longer time than this it is not lawful to steep it. At the expiration of the seventy days they wash the corpse, and wrap the whole body in bandages and flaxen cloth, smearing it with gum, which the Egyptians commonly use instead of glue.[6]

While there is much that is accurate in this description, recent studies have indicated that there were more steps to the mummification during the New Kingdom, for example, than are reflected here.

Embalming techniques were clearly sophisticated in ancient Egypt, but they never attained the level of perfection of other civilizations. Concerning oriental practices Ange-Pierre Leca notes:

The Chinese, for instance, knew how to keep the body supple and the features life-like and undistorted, and their knowledge was so advanced that the femoral artery of Prince Li-Chu-Tsang, whose two thousand one hundred year old body which has recently been discovered, is said to be still the same colour as it would be if it had just been removed from a newly-dead corpse.[7]

The general order of embalming may be constructed as follows:

Removal of the brain
Evisceration
First washing of the body
Treatment of the viscera
Dehydration of the corpse
Second washing
Stuffing of the body
Special treatment of the nails, eyes and external genital organs

The coffin of Djed-Khons-Iwef-Ank inside a hearse from McGorry Funeral Home on its way to St. Luke's Hospital in Cleveland for CAT scan and X-ray. *Photo by Mary Beth Camp, courtesy the Cleveland Health Education Museum and St. Luke's Hospital.*

Anointing and massaging the body after dehydration
Placing a covering on the side of the body
Final preparations before wrapping, treating the body with resin
Wrapping[8]

The embalming process in Egypt was carried out by a special class of workers who were both loved and hated by the general population. The profession was a hereditary one, according to Herodotus, and by all ancient accounts, not a pleasant one.

The embalmer's fingers are evil-smelling, for their odour is that of corpses. His eyes burn with the heat. He is too tired to stand up to his own daughter. He passes the day in cutting garments out of old rags for his clothing is an abomination to him.[9]

The mutilation of the human body, even for the lofty purposes of survival in the after-life, was repugnant to the sensitivities of the Egyptian. Even though the work of the em-

Above: A young adult man dating to the Roman Period. *Courtesy the British Museum.*

Left: A Greek youth, aged 19-21, discovered at Hawara (the Roman Period). The body is in a cartonnage case painted red with mythological scenes in gold-leaf. On the chest is the inscription, "O Artemidorus, farewell." *Courtesy the British Museum.*

balmer was executed far from the public eye, he was surrounded by official priests and readers whose job it was to
recite the traditional liturgies while he performed the various
operations. Word of his activities became common
knowledge as these who observed his work shared their
knowledge with family and friends. A number of assistants
were present for the work, and they would also circulate information on what the embalmer did to the body.

Adding to the dark reputation of these mummy makers
was the fact that a few unscrupulous types helped themselves
to the precious jewels and amulets supplied by the family
and, instead, packed small field stones in the linen wrapping.
Furthermore, there was the case of the embalmer who was
caught raping a woman's corpse, an event that apparently
had become so much of a problem that in later periods
women embalmers alone worked with the bodies of
women.[10]

Some of the work of the embalmers was sloppy, letting
tools, trash, even small animals get into the wrappings. The
attitude probably was, "What difference did it make? The
relatives of the dead man weren't going to unwrap him, and
nothing essential had been left out."[11]

Even more bizarre is the following situation described by
Barbara Mertz.

> More serious were cases like that of the woman whose in-
> ner workings had been lost or misplaced while the body was
> being mummified. The embalmer finally made up a set of
> organs out of a coil of rope and a bit of cowskin and some
> rags, bundled them up with the four sacred figures, and put
> them inside the lady. One would like to think that she en-
> countered him later, in the hereafter; their conversation
> would have been interesting to hear.[12]

A period of seventy days was required for both embalming and mourning. This is a time frame not only common
to Egyptian papyri, but is mentioned in the Old Testament

as well (Gen. 50:3). After the body was washed at the Purification Tent, it was taken to the Per-Nefer ("House of Mummification") where the brain was removed. The body was placed on an embalming table which, in some instances, measured seven feet long and five feet wide. The brain was removed through the left nostril with the use of hooks and probes. On rare occasions it was removed through a hole in the back of the head as in cases of King Ahmose and Waty.[13] For reasons not at all clear, the brain was evidently discarded, a procedure that must have been disconcerting to the educators of that day.

By means of a five-inch vertical incision in the left flank of the abdomen, the entrails of the body cavity were removed with the exception of the heart. Since the heart was considered to be the center of physical, emotional, and intellectual life, it had to remain intact.

Once the viscera were removed, they were washed and packed in natron, and treated with hot resin. After being wrapped, they were placed in four Canopic jars, each of which was guarded by one of the four sons of Horus. The lids on the vessels were formed into figures symbolizing these deities of the underworld. The intestines were placed in a jar with the head of a baboon representing the god Hapi. The falcon god, Qebehsenuf, guarded the liver, and the stomach was placed under the care of the god Amset, who was represented by the head of a man. Finally, the lungs were placed in a jar whose protection depended on the powers of the jackal-headed god, Duamutef.

The female genital organs were generally removed, but the male ones were left intact. The next and most crucial step in the process involved the dehydration of the body with the use of natron. This substance, composed of sodium carbonate and sodium bicarbonate, with sodium chloride and sodium sulfate as impurities, is found in a number of places in Egypt where it surfaces after standing waters have evaporated.

Older scholars had argued, following the suggestion of Herodotus, that the bodies were soaked or dipped in natron baths. Others have supposed that the bodies were dehydrated with the use of fire or treated with lime. The arguments against these suggestions are really quite compelling and the positive scientific evidence for dry natron is conclusive.

The absence of large containers with natron encrustation argues strongly against the general use of liquid natron for mummification. Recent tests conducted by A.T. Sandison of the Department of Pathology at the University of Glasgow have demonstrated rather clearly that dry natron best accounts for the results found in the mummies which presently exist. Sandison used both solutions of natron and dry natron in his experiments. His conclusion is significant.

> Preservation of human tissues with dry natron produces appearance reasonably similar to those seen in Egyptian mummies, allowing for the fact that after desiccation the latter were further treated, possibly with resins, etc. It is concluded that the evidence available from observational and experimental studies greatly favors the hypothesis that natron was used in solid form for mummification of the human body in ancient Egypt.[14]

Dry parcels of natron wrapped in linen were placed inside the body while the outside was covered with loose natron or packages of natron wrapped in linen. The warm, dry atmosphere of Egypt certainly accelerated the whole drying process.

Since 75 percent of the human body consists of water, this clearly was the biggest challenge in embalming technique. If this process could not be carried out efficiently, the flesh would decay, and further preservation would not be possible.

After the body was dehydrated, it was taken out of the natron, and the wet rags were removed and placed in jars.

The corpse was given a sponge bath with water and perhaps some perfumes. This part of the process took about forty days.

The skin was then anointed with resins and the body packed with linen soaked in the same material.

> At the end of the designated period the body emerged dry and desiccated, with loosened skin. It was at this point that the twenty-first dynasty embalmer departed from the practices of his predecessors and rose to heights of creative power. (Or, as Winlock puts it, he resorted to an expedient of somewhat doubtful taste.) He stuffed the body.[15]

Stuffing the body was not particularly new, but in the Twenty-first Dynasty slits were made in the skin and the mummy was actually padded with the use of sawdust, salt and other substances. This was an attempt to recreate the appearance the individual had in life.

During the Twenty-first Dynasty, the body was often painted and the face carefully adorned with cosmetics, even to the point of glueing on artificial eyebrows.

Before wrapping, the body was coated with molten resin to close the pores and protect the skin. It was this procedure, in addition to the special care given to the wrapping process, that accounted for the outstanding preservation of New Kingdom mummies. Upon completion of these steps, the body was then ready to be bound into that compact bundle we now call the mummy.

Linen cloth was almost always used in this process with the arms, legs and, in some periods, the fingers and toes being bound separately. Approximately twenty or more layers of alternating shrouds and bandages were wrapped around the entire body with coatings of resin interspersed. Considerable amounts of cloth were required for the normal wrapping as observed in one Eleventh Dynasty mummy that used 375 square meters. The linen employed for such wrapping purposes was not made especially for shrouds, but consisted of old household goods saved for this purpose.

Often the linen was marked with the name of the former owner or perhaps the name of the deceased. Small amulets, jewels and other objects were placed within the resins or wrappings of the mummy. Such objects can now be located and studied by x-ray without having to unwrap the body as was frequently done in the past. Many mummies were mutilated by tomb robbers in order to get such jewels and amulets.

There is convincing evidence that much of this robbery was carried out by the very priests who were charged with the responsibility of protecting these bodies. An American archaeologist, Herbert Winlock, observed that no gold was removed from any of the religious or royal symbols on the coffin. The sacred cobra carved on the rim of the Pharaoh's crown and the name of the god Ptah Sokar remained untouched when all other gold had been stripped away. Winlock suggested that discriminatory robbery could only

Model of a boat from the tomb of Khentikhety at Sedment. Courtesy of The University Museum, The University of Pennsylvania.

have been the work of knowledgeable priests.[16]

Recently, the University of Michigan conducted a series of x-ray studies of mummies in the Cairo Museum. In some cases artifacts and jewels were placed inside the body cavities which had been sewed up. Dr. James Harris, who directed the work, noted that approximately twenty percent of the mummies which had been in the museum since 1898 still had secret jewelry hidden in their burial wrappings and bodies.

When the wrapping of the body had been completed, the embalmer's shop was cleaned and all the embalming materials which had been in contact with the body were placed in jars for storage in the tomb. Occasionally these materials were buried separately as in the case of Tutankhamun. His cache of embalming materials was discovered in 1908 (fourteen years before his tomb) and included the remains of nine chickens, four geese, a shoulder of beef, sheep ribs and the floral collars worn by the mourners.[17]

Coffins

Egyptian coffins were usually made of wood, but under the Ptolemies and Romans hard stone was also employed. One of the oldest coffins in existence is probably that of Menkaure (Mycerinus) of the Fourth Dynasty. Now resting in the British Museum, this coffin was constructed of well-planed wood. Most coffins of the first six dynasties featured carved inscriptions in the cover and a human face. During the Eleventh and Twelfth Dynasties the coffin took a rectangular form with a cover consisting of a flat plank about two and one-half inches thick. The outside of the coffin was decorated with well-cut hieroglyphics, portions of which later became the "Book of the Dead." Inscriptions were also featured inside the coffin and related largely to magical texts which would provide protection in the after-life. On the out-

Above: New-born child found in Tarkhan (Roman Period). There is no evidence of disease. *Courtesy the British Museum.*

At right: The remains of a middle-aged man named Ankhef from the XI Dynasty. Studies have shown he suffered from osteo arthritis of the spine and the left hip. *Courtesy the British Museum.*

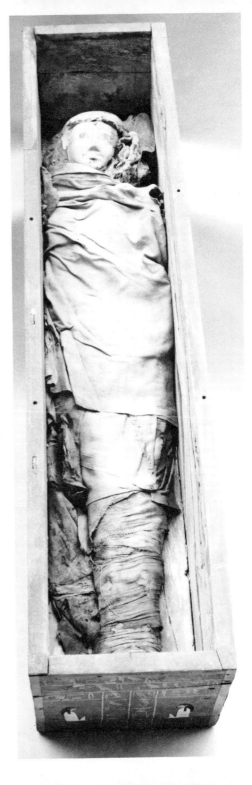

side of the coffin, opposite the place where the corpse's head would lie, were usually painted to udjat eyes. These appeared on the east side so the deceased could look out at the rising sun.[18] Prayers to the gods Anubis and Osiris were commonly painted on the west side of the coffin.

It was in the New Kingdom Period that the mummy-shaped coffins became common with the characteristic rounded shoulders and head. Like previous coffins, they were made of wood and painted inside and out, frequently in black. The face was gilded or colored a bright red, and the eyes were often inlaid. They were extremely attractive and very colorfully painted.

The Nineteenth Dynasty saw the rise of a new class of coffins which were some of the best ever produced. Decorated inside and out, the gods and selections from the Book of the Dead were portrayed in striking colors. From the Twenty-first Dynasty onward, coffins began to exhibit a great variety of individual tastes with some painted in black, while others were left in their natural color. White backgrounds were also popular with hieroglyphics represented in a variety of colors.

Starting with the Twenty-sixth Dynasty, the art of coffin making degenerated rapidly. Examples from this period are characteristically rough and represent careless workmanship. It is evident from the arrangement of scenes and the hieroglyphic inscriptions that those who painted them had little knowledge of their significance. Their efforts were crude imitations of earlier workmanship.

When the coffin was complete and the burial rites had been finished, it was usually placed in a sarcophagus. These large, rectangular stone repositories were made of either black or green basalt, granite, agglomerate or limestone. During the first six dynasties they were rectangular and the cover either flat or vaulted. The sarcophagus of Menkaure was found in his pyramid at Giza and resembled a small building.

It was beautifully sculptured but was without any ornamentation. The sarcophagi of this period usually had their sides made to represent the openings, vestibules and doors of the mastabas. If there were inscriptions upon them, they normally only contained the names or titles of their owners, and prayers that special gifts would be made to the deceased on specified festivals.

Little is known of the sarcophagi which were in use from the Seventh to the Tenth Dynasties. During the Eleventh and Twelfth Dynasties, rectangular wooden coffins seemed to have replaced, to some degree, the stone sarcophagi of the earlier periods. The shape and composition of sarcophagi from the Thirteenth to the Seventeenth are largely unknown. Eighteenth Dynasty sarcophagi, however, are frequently in the shape of a mummy, made of granite and very simply ornamented. This form of sarcophagi continued with minor changes throughout the Nineteenth Dynasty.

In the Twentieth Dynasty granite was commonly used for sarcophagi, but the form underwent considerable change. The deceased was usually represented on the lid, and there was a greater degree of individuality expressed. Coffins of this period through the Thirtieth Dynasty are of two types: ". . . those between the 22nd and 26th are shallower and smaller, while those of the 26th to the 30th are disproportionately broad so that the faces are grotesquely large. These faces are painted red, yellow or green, and underneath them appear the usual broad collar and pectoral."[19]

While the styles of the coffin and sarcophagus underwent change, their function remained the same, namely, to guarantee a secure and happy after-life.

The Mummification of Animals

Since virtually every animal in Egypt had some sort of religious significance, it comes as no surprise that many of them were mummified with the same particular care that

Mummified Ibis discovered in an Ibis Cemetary. Abydos. Dated to the Roman Period. *Courtesy of The Oriental Institute, University of Chicago.*

Mummified crocodile found in Shegilgil, Egypt. *Courtesy of the Oriental Institute, University of Chicago.*

A mummified cat from Beni Hasan, Egypt. *Courtesy of the Oriental Institute, University of Chicago.*

human bodies received. Mummified jackals, cats, ibises, snakes, lizards, gazelles, hawks, bulls, sheep, baboons, crocodiles and ducks have been found throughout the land. The most important animal, however, was the Apis bull who was venerated at Memphis.

> There was only one Apis bull at any given moment, and it was found by scouring Egypt for a male calf that was exactly the right colour, had precisely the right markings and scrupulously fulfilled various other religious and astrological stipulations. These made the right calf sacred, and from then on it was treated like a pharaoh for life, with priests and servants ministering to what they interpreted as its whims.[20]

When such sacred bulls died, they were accorded the same detailed embalming rites as would have been utilized on kings and queens. The importance of the Apis bull, considered to be the sacred animal of the god Ptah, is best illustrated by one of the most spectacular archaeological discoveries in the region of Memphis.

On November 13, 1856, Auguste Mariette found a shaft-like stairway leading to an underground avenue measuring 320 feet long. Later excavations revealed that the total length of the tunnel reached 1,120 feet. Using only torch lights, Mariette and a few of his workmen discovered sixty-four large burial chambers arranged along the avenue. Near the center of each burial room was a huge red or black granite sarcophagus approximately twelve feet long, nine feet high, and six feet wide, each weighing about sixty tons. In each of these a sacred Apis bull had been buried.

It was evident to Mariette as he moved around these rooms that they had long ago been robbed except for one chamber which had escaped the eyes of the treasure hunters. This chamber, sealed during the reign of Ramses II, is described by G. Frederick Owen.

> There, in the mortar was the imprint of the fingers of the mason who had set the last stone during the reign of Ramses II, and there in the dust were the footprints of those who

had trod the floor more than 3000 years ago. There also were the votive offerings dedicated by visitors who had come and gone so many centuries ago, among them an inscribed tablet of Ramses' own son, high priest of Apis, and one of the chief dignitaries of the time. It is little wonder that when the great explorer stood in this tomb and saw things as they had remained inviolate for some thirty-one eventful centuries he was overwhelmed and burst into tears.[21]

Since every animal was, in one way or other associated with a deity, the Egyptians not only mummified many of them, but also provided special cemeteries for their burial. Usually only one kind of animal was buried in a given cemetery, and a temple devoted to the cult of that animal was located adjacent to the cemetery.

At Sakkara a cemetery was found which had been devoted to baboons which were sacred to Thoth containing the mummified remains of 400 bodies. The Ibis bird was also sacred to Thoth, and cemeteries containing more than one-half million mummified birds have been discovered in the same region. These birds had been carefully wrapped in linen and then placed in sealed pottery jars which were stacked in rows in the galleries.

Also of special interest was the discovery of a mummified crocodile in which papyrus had been stuffed and used as exterior wrapping. The careful steaming of the papyrus leaves provided an interesting ink-written Greek Text.

A similar text was recovered from a third century B.C. human mummy found at Ghoran. The frugal embalmers at this site, like others of the period, used discarded scraps of papyrus to make mummy coffins and to wrap the corpse. A team of French specialists used a steaming technique and a mixture of hydrochloric acid and warm water to get to the precious papyrus. As the resin materials were broken down by the acid, they could be brushed away thus exposing the papyrus which was then separated by the warm steam. It is believed that part of the document recovered may be a copy of a play written around 300 B.C. by the Greek poet, Menander.[22]

A careful study of mummified animal forms by means of x-ray reveals the fact that great numbers of mummiform animals were actually fakes. While the exteriors were elaborately wrapped and decorated, they contained nothing inside. Illustrations of this practice are found in abundance from the seventh century B.C. to the first century A.D. Apparently these animals were in such demand that domestic farming could not produce them in sufficient quantities.

It is possible that such animal-form burials were just symbolic in nature so that each family could be properly represented at the sacred cemetery. In this case, it would not have been imperative that an actual body be in the casing. The function of that magical form would have been just like the numerous statues that were placed in the tomb, that is, to provide for the needs of the deceased in the after-life.

Of course, ancient embalmers were not above the economic attractiveness of mass producing "sacred mummies" for a religious minded public. The enterprising embalmer could mass produce these mummified animal forms in a very short period of time and, without the presence of the modern x-ray, no one would be the wiser.

For the paleo-biologist, the discovery of mummified animals is of special interest not only from an ecological standpoint, but it provides a means of comparison with the repertoire of animals appearing in tomb paintings. Such information is invaluable in reconstructing the ecological systems of ancient Egypt.

Significant Burial Objects

Associated with the mummy in the tomb were a number of objects which in almost all cases, had practical functions in the after-life. Already mentioned were the four Canopic jars which contained the principal organs of the deceased.

The name "Canopic" originated with Egyptologists who believed that the jars confirmed the legend handed down by ancient writers that Osiris was worshipped at Canopus (a port situated at the mouth of the Nile) in the form of a vase with a stopper shaped like Osiris' head.

These four funerary urns came into use as early as the

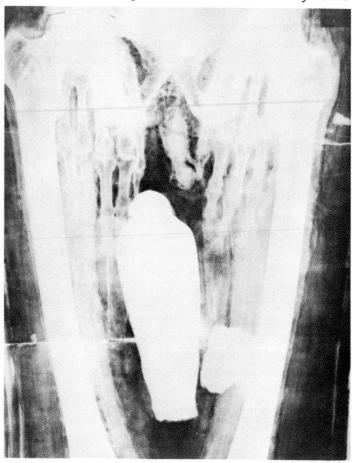

A radiograph of the upper legs of a middle aged man. Note the pottery ushabi-figure between the bones. The hands are also visible in the picture. *Courtesy the British Museum.*

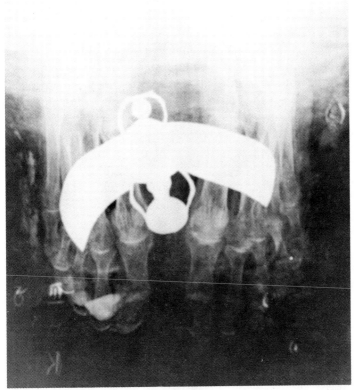

Radiograph of the feet of a priestess aged 25-40 in cartonnage casing named Tjent-mulengebtiu (XXI Dynasty). Across the feet lies a pectoral, perhaps of metal, in the form of a winged scarabaeus holding the sun's disc between its front legs and a smaller disc between its hind legs. *Courtesy the British Museum.*

Third Dynasty when they were placed on a ledge hollowed out in the south end of the tomb's antechamber or in a second sarcophagus which stood next to the one containing the mummy. During the Fifth Dynasty and following, they were placed in a four-compartment chest which was located next to the sarcophagus. Such Canopic chests were sometimes placed on top of a small sled with two runners.

Most of them are only two feet square and decorated with four deities.

In the later periods (Twenty-sixth Dynasty and following), the traditional use of Canopic jars came to an end and the entrails of the individual were either placed between the legs or in the body cavity. The importance of the tradition persisted, however, and "false" Canopic jars were produced which have a shaped exterior but were never hollowed out for actual use. Apparently the Egyptian felt that it was necessary to guarantee protection of the organs by means of the Canopic jars. Still later, the use of the jars was abandoned altogether.

Another collection of funerary objects of equal importance to a proper burial was the Ushabti or Shantis figures. The typical Ushabti figure was that of man in mummiform with his hands crossed and often holding a pair of shoes. Sometimes a seed basket, brick mold, or pair of buckets would be painted on the back of such figures. Some statues have even been found wearing clothes. Royal Ushabti figures were frequently made of gold or finely carved stone.

It is believed by many that the word "ushabti" (also spelled shabti, shawabti or washabti) had been associated with the

Typical Canopic jars bearing the heads of the Four Sons of Horus. From the left: Hapi (to guard the lungs), Qebhsnve (to guard the intestines), Duamutef (to guard the stomach), and Imsem (to guard the liver). *Photo by the author.*

Pottery and wooden Ushabtis of the XVIII Dynasty. *Courtesy of the Oriental Institute, University of Chicago.*

word *washab,* meaning "answerer." In other words, this model with magical power could answer to the needs of the deceased in the after-life and by that, eliminate the possibility that he would be a working servant in the land beyond the river.

While these figures see their prominent use during the Middle Kingdom Period and following, the root idea was extant in funerary tradition of the Old Kingdom when so-called "reserve heads" were buried with the dead. It was believed that if the actual head of the mummy should be destroyed, these could take over. Apparently such magical

A young male child from the Roman Period. *Courtesy the British Museum.*

A female child with the head flexed (the Roman Period). Abdominal cavities appear to be empty. All bones are normal and free from fractures, dislocations and disease. *Courtesy The British Museum.*

power was later attributed to the statues with a whole body and then, at a later time, to the Ushabti models.

Important light is shed on the function of the Ushabti by the papyrus of Nebseni which is preserved in the British Museum.

> The scribe Nebseni, the draughtsman in the temples of the north and south, the man highly venerated in the temple of Ptah, saith: "Oh thou shabti figure of the scribe Nebseni, the son of the scribe of Thena, justified, and of the lady of the house of Mutrestha, justified, if I be called, or if I be adjudged to do any work whatsoever of the labors which are to be done in the underworld . . . let the judgment fall upon thee instead of upon me always, in the matter of sowing the fields, of filling the water courses with water, and of bringing the sands of this east to the west."
> The shabti figure answereth, "Verily I am here, and will come withersoever thou biddest me."[23]

In addition to the Ushabtis, other figurines possessing magical powers were wood models of human figures engaged in various activites of domestic life such as fishing, bread making, butchering cattle, and brewing beer. Such models would guarantee that the various needs of the deceased would be met by these servants. Prior to the New Kingdom Period, these servants were normally represented by painted figures on the tomb walls.

Royal tombs were also outfitted with furniture, clothing, sandals, jewelry, a variety of food, and other articles which would provide for suitable living in the after-life. Jars of wine, beer, and water, along with dishes or trays of bread, roast duck, dried fish, figs and dates were all part of the necessary assemblage for the deceased.

Also in great abundance were the amulets and scarabs which afforded additional protection for the mummy. Hundreds of different amulets existed, each with some special function. Normally, these were supplied by the embalmer, but they could also be provided by relatives and friends of the deceased.

Middle Kingdom burials of the poor have yielded crudely made clay model houses commonly called "soul houses." Not able to afford the more expensive Ushabti figures, they assumed that these model houses would provide a resting place for the man's Ka and food for his survival.

Model boats discovered in the tombs are of two types. One type depicts a funeral barge with a mummy on a bier which was supposed to take the deceased to the underworld of Osiris, and the other, represents simple Nile activities such as fishing.

These objects, along with the elaborate tombs in which they were found, continue to capture the imagination of the observer. Additionally, the recent medical studies on the actual bodies of the Pharaohs and other mummies have opened up exciting horizons of information which breathe new life into the study of ancient Egyptian culture.

5 New Light On Old Bones

Few things have been the subject of more romantic dreaming than the mummies of ancient Egypt. The astonishing discoveries of these individuals in the dark tomb chambers along the Nile have only increased interest in the land of the Nile.

For decades historians have been able to analyze Egyptian records and archaeologists have uncovered the ruins of ancient cities, but it has only been in recent years that medical specialists have taken a close look at the anatomical character of these peoples.

The current medical examination of Egypt's mummies has involved multidisciplinary teams utilizing x-ray units, radiograms, electron microscopes, polytomography, amino acid racemization reaction, and atomic absorbtion tests, to name just a few. Dating the bodies has been based on carbon-14 tests, art and inscriptional analysis of coffin texts and amino acid racemization reaction factors.

Disciplines now being utilized in the study of mummified

humans include medicine, physical anthropology, Egyptology, pathology, parasitology, physiology, radiology, electron microscopy, microbiology and dentistry.

Many mummies cannot be unwrapped for direct physical examination, so x-rays must be utilized, and they have proven most useful and, at times, embarrassing. For example, a wrapped mummy was found buried with Makare and originally labeled by museum personnel as being "Princess Moutemhet." After an x-ray was taken, it was discovered that the mummy was that of female hamadryas baboon![1] It is now known that the name Moutemhet belongs to Makare herself.[2]

The earliest systematic examination of the mummy collection in Cairo was undertaken by the French Egyptologist Gaston Maspero in 1889, which was followed by the work of anatomist Grafton Elliot Smith. To really achieve accurate medical conclusions regarding these bodies, however, they needed not only to be x-rayed, but unwrapped and parts of the body dissected for microscopic examination. These early scholars had too deep a respect for the Egyptian craft of mummification and the value of the mummified form to destroy any part of the body. Needless to say, many of their conclusions regarding these mummies need to be reevaluated in the light of more modern studies.

Two common questions raised concerning these studies are: why are they undertaken and what results are anticipated? There are several answers which really address both inquiries.

First, such studies will aid in the verification of historical data. For example, it is well known that some battles were fought between the native Egyptian rulers at Thebes and the Hyksos to the north. Historians have long suspected an armed conflict between Seqenenre Tao, a Seventeenth Dynasty ruler and the Hyksos king, Apophis.

When the mummified head of Seqenenre Tao was unwrapped, it was evident that he had suffered a violent death.

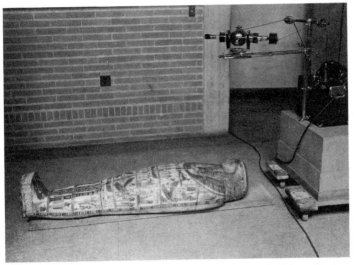

Mummy in anthropoid coffin is ready for x-ray analysis by Dr. J. G. Cohen. *Courtesy The University Museum, The University of Pennsylvania.*

A horizontal ax wound and a large hole made by a blunt instrument in the forehead were easily discernible. The cheekbone of the king had also been completely shattered by a violent blow.

A severe wound had also been made deep in the back of his neck by a dagger, perhaps indicating that he had been attacked from behind or while lying down.[3] While it is entirely possible that he was the victim of a court assassination, the poor condition of the head and crude wrapping would seem to argue that he had died in battle. Indications are that his head and body had been retrieved some distance from the royal palace and the embalmers.

Relationships between members of the royal household have always been a complex matter for historians to untangle due to intermarriage among family members as well as foreigners. X-ray studies, in addition to anatomical examination, have helped to clarify some of the knotty problems.

A classical example of such study is the work of Professor

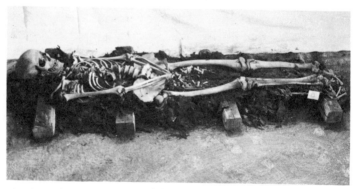

Three stages in the unwrapping of a 600 B.C. mummy from Tomb 314 at Meydum.
Courtesy The University Museum, The University of Pennsylvania.

James Harris, Chairman of the Department of Orthodonics at the University of Michigan and Professor Kent R. Weeks, Chairman of the Department of Anthropology at the American University in Cairo. By careful x-ray techniques and visual examination they were able to gather an enormous amount of vital medical information concerning Egypt's royal mummies.

Some of the mummies recovered from the Deir el-Bahri cache had not been identified by earlier scholars, but based on anatomical analysis, proposed identifications were suggested by Weeks and Harris.

An example of this detective work is a lady labeled as "Unknown Woman B," who stood about 5'2" tall with artificial braids intertwined with her own white hair to hide a noticeable degree of baldness.[4] After examination of the physical characteristics of the mummy, they plausably suggested that she was Tetisheri, mother of Ahhotep and the grandmother of Ahmose-Nefertiry. Most significant, however, is her identification as the wife of Seqenenre Tao of the Seventeenth Dynasty. The Michigan expedition x-ray studies also revealed the following:

> Her head broken from the badly damaged body, was one of the first studies. X-rays showed the same prominent dentition, the same type of malocclusion, and same shape of skull as the women found in the royal caches of the next four generations. The moderate wear on her teeth and even an impacted third molar, which lay at a very disfunctional angle in the jaw, were the same sort of problems found among her descendants.[5]

Other fascinating types of information on the royal mummies include the revelation that King Ahmose I, the son of Seqenenre Tao (unlike most Egyptian males) was not circumcised.[6] The authors suggest that the Pharaoh was probably in ill health and may have been a hemophiliac or "bleeder."[7]

The chest x-ray of Meryet-Amon, the wife and sister of Amen-hotep I, reveals conditions of arthritis and scoliosis (an abnormal curvature of the spine).[8] Many of the royal mummies exhibit extreme wear of tooth enamel, especially those of advanced age. Such wear is normally attributed to the presence of tiny chips of stone in ground flour.

An anatomic analysis of the body of Thutmoses II revealed that he died at about 30 years of age and was a very frail individual who had suffered disease for a significant period prior to his death.[9]

It should be observed at this point, that the medical study of mummies has benefits that extend beyond historical concerns.

> Yet the nature of diseases prevalent thousands of years ago in ancient Egypt is not solely a matter of academic interest, but is of practical importance, for in many instances the eradication of a disease may not be achieved until the way in which it evolved has been determined.[10]

The Manchester Project

The employment of the x-ray also proved valuable in the Manchester Museum Mummy Project headed by A. Rosalie David, Assistant Keeper of Archaeology at the Manchester Museum in Manchester, England. In 1975 a highly specialized interdisciplinary team was drawn from various departments of the university to examine Mummy No. 1770.

The purpose of the examination was to determine the physical and dental health of this mummy and attempt to discern the presence of disease and perhaps the cause of death. The results were very successful and led to the convening of the First International Symposium on Mummies at Manchester, England.[11]

The Manchester project focused on the mummy of Artemidora revealing that she was in her sixties at death. This hitherto unknown fact was established by the bone structure and signs of calcification of the femoral arteries.[12]

Another mummy by the name Nakhtankh revealed that he had suffered lesions of certain blood vessels by constantly inhaling sand particles. This was discovered when a section

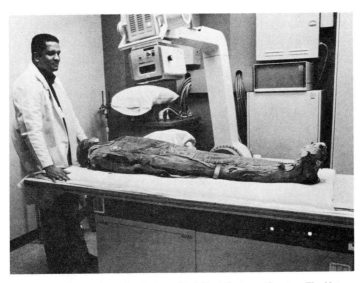

Dr. Charles White prepares the mummy, Djed-Hapi, for x-ray. *Courtesy The University Museum, The University of Pennsylvania.*

was made from his lungs which were preserved in one of the canopic jars, and magnified 120 times under an electron microscope.

Adding to our knowledge of the Egyptian mummy was the work conducted at Wayne State University School of Medicine on a mummy known as Pum II. The mummy had been loaned to Wayne State from the collection at the University of Pennsylvania Museum.

After an autopsy was performed, it was first speculated that the body dated back to 700 B.C., but upon further examination and tests, the date of 170 B.C. has now been established. The man, who stood 5'4" tall, died sometime between his 35th and 40th birthdays.

Examination of the head indicated that the right ear drum had been perforated, suggesting that he had suffered from some ear inflamation. Of special interest was the existence of a mummified insect in the form of a small beatle larvae which was found inside the ear.

Unwrapping the mummy for anatomic examination was no small task because the body had been wrapped in 12 layers of linen over which hot liquid resin had been liberally poured.[13] Sections of the covering had to be removed with chisel or cut through several layers at a time with a Stryker saw.[14]

Once the skin of the mummy had been exposed to air, it began to change color. In fact, the body turned from a light brown to a darker brown within twenty-four hours. Today the skin is almost a black-brown.[15]

Studies such as the one above continue to shed fascinating light on the world of the ancient Egyptian. Conclusions regarding their diet, types of work and causes of death can now be determined with reasonable accuracy. Such information creates a special sense of historical reality and enhances our

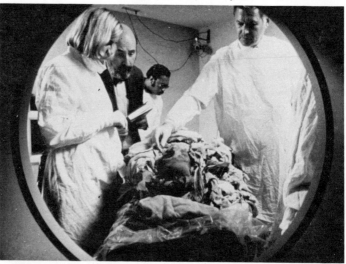

The Egyptian priest, Djed-Khons-Iwef-Ankh, is the center of attention in the CAT scan room at St. Luke's Hospital in Cleveland. The mummy was on loan to St. Luke's Hospital from Western Reserve Historical Society for medical study. *Photograph by Mary Beth Camp. Courtesy of Cleveland Health Education Museum and St. Luke's Hospital.*

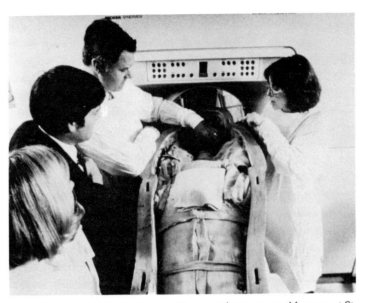

Djed-Khons-Iwef-Ankh, a 3000-year-old priest, is being prepared for x-ray at St. Luke's Hospital in Cleveland. *Photo by Mary Beth Camp. Courtesy the Cleveland Health Education Museum and St. Luke's Hospital.*

understanding of the ancient world.

One more project worthy of note in the medical study of mummies was recently undertaken at St. Luke's Hospital in Cleveland under the direction of Dr. Jerald S. Brodkey. The mummy, which was identified as Djed-Khons-Iwef-Anekh, was x-rayed and CAT-scanned.[16]

Studies on this mummy, who was embalmed approximately 1000 B.C., revealed the presence of a number of amulets made of faience as well as stones under the eyelids.[17] Analysis of the x-rays and CAT-scans is continuing at Ohio State University.

Not all medical studies provide such positive information leading to the resolution of historical problems, however. For example, Pharaoh Ramses II was supposed to have ruled for at least sixty-seven years according to historical documents, but when his mummy was examined, it was discovered that his biological age at death could not have been more than fifty-nine years! A whole host of explanations have appeared to try to resolve this difficulty, but none is convincing. It is now evident that the historians and medical specialists will need to work more closely in the years ahead in order to provide conclusions that are in closer agreement.

Mummy Powder Medicine

Thieves, both ancient and modern, have entered the royal tombs, and it was not uncommon for them to hack in pieces the mummified bodies of royalty in order to retrieve precious objects and to dispell the curse they felt might fall on them. But the destruction of the precious mummies' form did not end there, unfortunately. In the thirteenth century A.D. and following, physicians actually prescribed "mummy powder" for a variety of ailments including epilepsy, heart murmurs, nausea, poisoning, paralysis, cuts, bruises, and tuberculosis. By the latter part of the sixteenth century, extensive trade had developed between Egypt and druggists in Europe. Mummies, both human and animal, were ground into powder, smuggled out of the land and sold to European druggists at exorbitant prices.

A tradition states that a fourteenth century A.D. physician named Elmagar, a native of Alexandria, was one of the first to prescribe mummy podwer for various ailments.[18] It was argued that the asphalt and bitumen consolidated and healed broken and lacerated veins.

The demand for mummy medication was greatest in France. Francois I, according to early records, was in the habit of always carrying with him a little packet containing some mummy powder mixed with pulverized rhubarb. This was supposed to protect him against injury and subsequent infection.[19]

With time it was quite evident that the demand for mummy powder would far exceed the ability of native Egyptians to provide it. As a result, all sorts of powder was produced from a variety of organic materials and sold to willing European merchants as "mummy powder."

> Some Jews entered upon a speculation to furnish the mummy thus brought into demand as an article of commerce, and undertook to embalm dead bodies and to sell them to the Christians. They took all the executed criminals and bodies of all descriptions that could be obtained, filled the head and inside of the bodies with simple asphaltum, an article of very small price, made incisions into the muscular parts of the limbs, inserted into them also the asphaltum and then bound them up tightly. This being done, the bodies were exposed to the heat of the sun: they dried quickly and resembled in appearance the truly prepared mummies. These were sold to the Christians.[20]

Happily, with the advance of enlightened medical studies combined with rigid legal controls imposed by Egypt, this traffic has largely ceased. Evidently, however, a small remnant remains who persist in using "mummy powder" for medical or magical purposes. There is a New York pharmacy that caters to customers who want genuine powdered Egyptian mummy. The cost is set at $40.00 an ounce.[21]

The desecration of the Egyptian mummy has a long and dark history. Even when the royal mummies are accorded careful scientific treatment, there is still an ethical and religious question that must be answered, because the object of one's study is, after all, the remains of a human being. Undoubtedly it is this latter factor that has recently caused the mummy room on the second floor of the museum in Cairo to be closed. The decision was clearly influenced by the rise of conservative Islamic power.

Even though the doors to the mummy room of the museum are closed, the world's fascination with these ancient Egyptians will continue. Only time will tell what new medical or historical information will emerge to change modern viewpoints on these peoples.

6 Mummification and the Bible

The well-known story of Joseph recorded in the latter chapters of the Book of Genesis provides for us two fascinating references to the embalming of the body. In Genesis 50:2-3 we read, "And Joseph commanded his servants, the physicians to embalm his father: and the physicians embalmed Israel. And forty days were fulfilled for him; for so are fulfilled the days of them which are embalmed; and the Egyptians mourned for him three score and ten days." Later in that same chapter reference is made to the death of Joseph and his subsequent embalming. Verse twenty-six reads as follows: So Joseph died, being 110 years old: and they embalmed him and he was put in a coffin in Egypt."

These quotations raise a series of intriguing questions. First, there is the matter of historical context. Under whose reign did Joseph live and rise to a position second only to the king? Who actually embalmed the body of Jacob and what methods were employed? Finally, there is the question of accuracy. Does the text of Genesis provide a reliable description of the embalming and mummification process?

The historical context of Joseph's appearance in Egypt has long been the subject of heated debate. The concensus of modern scholarship is that Joseph arrived in Egypt and rose to power during the days of Hyksos rulers. This view is established on two basic arguments. The first is an assertion of Josephus drawn from Manetho, that Joseph was in Egypt under Hyksos rule. The second argument is based on the opinion that it would be more likely for a Semite or Asiatic to rise to a position of prominence as Joseph did under Semitic Hyksos rulers rather than native Egyptians.

If one takes biblical data seriously, however, it would appear that Joseph migrated into Egypt approximately 1875 B.C. Since Joseph had already been there for some time, a Middle Kingdom date for his sale into Egyptian slavery and his rise to prominence seems to be required.[1] The Bible places the exodus of the Israelites from Egypt approximately 1445 B.C. This date is established by adding 480 years to the fourth year of Solomon mentioned in I Kings 6:1. According to Exodus 12:40, Jacob and his descendants came down to Egypt 430 years before the great exodus. This then would place the rise of Joseph to power in Egypt some time after 1875 B.C. and would, therefore, require his presence in Egypt during the Middle Kingdom period under native Egyptian Pharaohs rather than the rulers of the Hyksos.

According to Battenfield, it was Sesostris II who first imprisoned, then later elevated Joseph to a position of power approximately 1884 B.C.; but since that Pharaoh died in 1878 B.C., Joseph's career falls largely in reign of King Sesostris III.[2]

There are a number of knotty problems that follow this chronology, however. Perhaps the most complex is the use of the word Potiphar as a proper name in Genesis 37:36. Most are agreed that this is the equivalent of the Egyptian *pa-di-pa-Ra,* meaning "the one whom (the god) Re has given".[3] The problem surrounding this word is the presence of the Egyptian definite article which occurs twice.

> The use of *pa* in personal names is almost, but not totally, a late development, rarely occurring in the Middle Kingdom. Hermann Franke in his authoritative study of Egyptian personal names lists 727 names with *pa* as the first element; of these only 15 date from earlier than the New Kingdom. A name beginning with *pa* is therefore unlikely, but not impossible in the Middle Kingdom.[4]

Of the many solutions offered for this difficult problem, Charles Aling's appears to be the most acceptable. It is his contention that the word "Potiphar" was used as a descriptive epithet meaning "one who is placed on earth by Re" (i.e. an Egyptian), and not as a name at all.[5]

This scene from the tomb of Sennefer, Thebes, depicts servants carrying funerary furniture. Gifts included sandals, a piece of linen, Ushabti figures, a gilded mask and the heart, the symbol of eternity. From the reign of Amenhotep II.

The evidence connecting Joseph with the Middle Kingdom period is indeed quite substantial and growing thanks to the efforts of Aling and others.[6] For example, Joseph's career as a household slave in Egypt as recorded in Genesis 39:2, 3 is now amply confirmed as a normative Middle Kingdom experience. Middle Kingdom inscriptions list such Asiatic slaves and of forty-eight listed, only six have specific titles. Four are designated cupbearers or butlers, and two are listed as domestic servants, thus reflectng a similar position as Joseph.[7]

When Joseph was required to present himself before Pharaoh, the scripture points out that he shaved himself as a necessary part of his preparation for that event (Gen. 41:14). This requirement is well understood in light of native Egyptian customs during the Middle Kingdom, but one wonders what significance such as an act would have with respect to a Semitic Hyksos ruler who would never have objected to beards. Furthermore, the elevation of Joseph and the official recognition of that event reflects typically Egyptian customs and practices (Gen. 41:38-44).

Further evidence that Joseph was in Egypt during the Middle Kingdom comes from the information found in Genesis 43:32. It is there noted that it was an abomination for the Egyptians to eat with the Hebrews. This observation would be strange indeed if Hyksos Pharaohs were in command during that time. The Hyksos, as we now know, were largely made up of Semitic rulers. Such a restriction would be difficult to correlate with Semitic rule, but is easily understood if native Middle Kingdom Pharaohs are in command.

Finally, the expression referring to Egyptian aversion to shepherds is further evidence for a native Egyptian context for Joseph's story. In Genesis 46:34 instruction is given that the brothers of Joseph were to identify themselves as herdsmen rather than shepherds ". . . for every shepherd is an abomination to the Egyptians." These references, in addi-

Model of a granary from the tomb of Khentikhety at Sedment. *Courtesy The University Museum, The University of Pennsylvania.*

tion to the biblical chronology, appear to place Joseph in the Middle Kingdom of Egyptian history. In the light of this, the verses of Genesis 50 relating to the death of Jacob and Joseph and their subsequent preparation for burial become important.

Physicians and Embalmers

We now come to the description of Jacob's death and embalming. It should be noted that Joseph designated "physicians" to care for the embalming of his father (Gen. 50:2). The Hebrew word for physicians in this text is *hāropeʾîm* which comes from the verbal root *rāpāʾ* meaning "to heal".[8] This is a common word used elsewhere to refer specifically to physicians whose concern were with the living and the healing of various illnesses. Why then should this Hebrew term be used to describe the embalming process? There were a number of other Hebrew words that could more specifically describe the traditional embalmer or mortician. There are two possibilities here. First, the term "physician" may be used here in the broadest sense of those who worked with the human body. The problem with this assumption is that among Egyptian professionals, the embalmers and the physicians were members of distinctly different classes.

More likely, Joseph intentionally called for physicians to prepare the body of his father in order to avoid the magical and mystical practices that would inevitably be part of the process if undertaken by Egyptian embalmers and priests.

Also of importance with respect to Genesis 50:2 is the use of word "embalm." This is a translation of the Hebrew *hānaṭ* meaning "to spice, make spicy, embalm."[9] The term is widely used for the preparation and use of spices. However, as it appears in the three verses in Genesis 50, it obviously applies to the preparation of the human body for death, perhaps with the use of spices, but certainly with other elements as well.

The actual time of the embalming and mourning is another important detail of the Genesis narrative. According to Genesis 50:3 the Egyptians "mourned for him three score and ten days." What exactly was included in this 70 day period? Some have seen contradictions at this point since in Egyptian documents the period of time involved in the

Left: An infant in cartonnage case from Beni Hasan (XXII Dynasty). The radiograph reveals the disorganized bones of an infant who suffered from a rare bone disorder. *Courtesy The British Museum.*

Right: A man, aged 40-50. A gilded cartonnage mask with beard covers the head. The body is overlaid with a bead-net. The mummy was discovered in Akhmim and dates back to the Ptolemaic Period. *Courtesy The British Museum.*

embalming process varies from one document to another. For example, in one case the embalming occupied 16 days; the bandaging 35 days; and the burial 70 days; i.e., 121 days in all. In another example the embalming took 66 days; special preparations for burial, 4 days; and the burial itself 26 days; in other words, a total of 96 days.[10] These cases, however, appear to have been exceptions to the normal practice.

Of great importance is the fact that in Egyptian documents there is constant reference to a period of 70 days which elapsed between the time of death and the completion of burial rites. No less than 5 Egyptian texts refer to this 70 day period, including a Ptolemaic Stela in the British Museum (No. 378), which reads ". . . he had a goodly burial after the 70 days of his embalming had been fulfilled."[11] Stela numbers 110 and 164, dating back to the Eighteenth Dynasty, also make reference to the same time period for the completion of the mummification process. One reference is from the reign of Queen Hatshepsut and the other from her successor, Thutmoses III. The relevant part of the inscription is the same in both cases reading: "A goodly burial arrives in peace, thy 70 days having been fulfilled in the place of embalming."[12]

The historian Herodotus suggested that it took 70 days to dehydrate the body, but later studies have shown this to be incorrect. More likely, the 70 day period includes 40 days for the dehydration process, and the remaining time for wrapping and final ceremonies. This accords very well with the embalming details of Jacob.

The principal time for dehydration and the beginning of wrapping would be approximately 40 days with the remaining 30 to include final wrapping, preparation of the coffin and a period of mourning followed by the delivery of the body.[13] These conclusions are further confirmed by Egyptologist Alfred Lucas who conducted a series of experiments involving dehydration and use of natron. His experiments have recently been confirmed by the work of Dr. Zaki Iskander in Cairo. Both reached the conclusion that the overall period of embalming, wrapping and mourning was approximately 70 days.[14]

It would be expected that Joseph, in holding such a high position in the land, would have accorded his father the best embalming possible by mummification, but certainly would have excluded the magical texts involving polytheism which would have necessarily accompanied traditional rites by native Egyptian embalmers.

Great Faith

When Joseph died at 110 years of age the biblical text indicates that he was also embalmed and put in a coffin in Egypt (Gen. 50:26). The word for coffin here is the Hebrew *aron*, meaning a chest or ark. This is the same word that is employed to describe the ark of the covenant in the Old Testament. Its use here, of course, refers to the coffin in which the body of Joseph was placed after embalming.

So great was Joseph's faith in the promise of the land that he requested that his bones be taken from the land of Egypt to Canaan when the children of Israel left Egypt (vv. 24-25, cf. Heb. 11:22). His mummy case or coffin remained with the Israelites throughout the 40 years wandering in the

Mummy from the 12th Dynasty. *Courtesy The Metropolitan Museum of Art. The Rogers Fund, 1912.*

wilderness (Exod. 13:19) and was later buried in Shechem (Josh. 24:32).

The faith of both Jacob and Joseph in the faithfulness of their God was not only eloquently exhibited in life, but reflected in the patterns of death and burial. Among the ancient peoples of Egypt and Palestine, the place of burial was always significant. Because of the localized nature of Egyptian deities, a native would consider it unthinkable to be buried in the soil of a foreign land. This is very amply reflected in the concerns of Sinuhe, an Egyptian official of the Middle Kingdom who went into voluntary exile in Asia. One of the concerns in having him returned to Egypt is that he would be properly buried in Egyptian soil.[15] The ancient Egyptian believed that their deities only had full power in the actual soils of the homeland. This is why Naaman, the Syrian, when healed, took "two mules-burden of earth" back to his homeland. He wanted to worship the Lord of the Hebrews (II Kings 5:17).

Recognition of this principle is also very significant in capturing the charm and sincerity of Ruth's testimony. Her words, "where thou diest, will I die and there will I be buried . . ." (Ruth 1:17) reflect a complete abandonment of Moab and its deities. Had she entertained lingering affections for the gods of Moab, she would have requested a burial in her land of birth in order to enjoy the protection of those deities.

The willingness of Joseph and Jacob to be buried in Canaan constitutes irrefutable evidence that they had not become worshipers of any of the Egyptian deities, but remained faithful to the God of their fathers.

Documentation

Chapter 1

[1]James Hamilton-Patterson and Carol Andrews, *Mummies: Death and Life in Ancient Egypt* (Middlesex, England: Penguin Books Ltd., 1978), p.184.

[2]Giovanni B. Belzoni, "Narrative of Operations and Recent Researches in Egypt and Nubia, 1820," reprinted in *Hands on the Past*, ed. by C. W. Ceram (New York: Alfred A. Knopf, 1966), p. 141.

[3]James Baikie, *A Century of Excavation in the Land of the Pharaohs* (London: Religious Tract Society, 1924), p. 12.

[4]Giovanni B. Belzoni, *op. cit.*, p. 140.

[5]*Ibid.*, p. 141.

[6]Gaston Maspero, "A Hoard of Royal Mummies," *Institut Egyptian Bulletin*, series 2, n. 2 (1881), trans. by P.A. Clayton, reprinted in *Hands on the Past*, op. cit., pp. 152-153.

[7]Hames Hamilton-Peterson and Carol Andrews, *op. cit.*, p. 156.

Chapter 2

[1]John A. Wilson, *The Culture of Ancient Egypt* (Chicago: the University of Chicago Press, 1951), p. 86.

[2]Henri Frankfort, *Ancient Egyptian Religion* (New York: Harper & Brothers, 1961), pp. 96-97.

[3]Pierre Montet, *Eternal Egypt* (New York: The American Library, 1964), p. 201.

[4]Henri Frankfort, *op. cit.*, p. 100.

[5]E. A. Wallis Budge, *The Mummy* (New York: Biblo and Tannen, 1964), p. 172.

[6]Adolf Erman, *The Ancient Egyptians*, trans. by A. M. Blackman (New York: Harper & Row, 1966), pp. 23-24.

[7]E. A. Wallis Budge, *op. cit.,* p. 172.

[8]James Baikie, *Egyptian Papri and Papyrus-Hunting* (New York: Fleming H. Revell Co., n.d.), p. 209.

Chapter 3

[1]Ange-Pierre Leca, *The Egyptian Way of Death,* trans. by Louise Asmal (Garden City; Doubleday & Company, Inc., 1981), p. 29.

[2]A. J. Spencer, *Death in Ancient Egypt* (New York: Penguin Books, 1982), p. 15.

[3]Adolf Erman, *op. cit.,* p. 237.

[4]James B. Pritchard, ed., *Ancient Near Eastern Texts,* "The Conquest of Death," trans. by John A. Wilson (Princeton: Princeton University Press, 1955,), p. 32 (hereafter referred to as ANET).

[5]Henri Frankfort, *op. cit.,* p. 93.

[6]*Ibid.*

[7]ANET, "Curses and Threats," trans. by John A. Wilson, p. 327.

[8]Fred G. Bratton, *A History of Egyptian Archaeology* (New York: Thomas Y. Crowell Co., 1968), p. 131.

[9]James Baikie, *Egyptian Papyri and Papyrus-Hunting,* p. 94.

[10]*Ibid.,* p. 87.

[11]John A. Wilson, *The Culture of Ancient Egypt,* pp. 54-55.

[12]On the whole issue of ancient numerology see, John J. Davis, *Biblical Numerology* (Grand Rapids: Baker Book House, 1968).

[13]Kurt Mendelssohn, *The Riddle of the Pyramids* (New York: Praeger Publishers, 1974), p. 143.

[14]*Ibid.,* pp. 141-142.

[15]John A. Wilson, *The Culture of Ancient Egypt,* p. 109.

Chapter 4

[1]E. A. Wallis Budge, *op. cit.,* p. 175.

[2]For a detailed study of these discoveries see P. V. Glob, *The Bog People,* trans. by Rupert Bruce-Mitford (Ithaca, N.Y.: Cornell University Press, 1969).

[3]Photographs of these mummies may be seen in Archie Lieberman and Ray Bradburg, *The Mummies of Guanajuato* (New York: Harry N. Abrams, 1974).

[4]Barbara Adams, *Egyptian Mummies* (London: Shire Publications, 1984), p. 21.

[5]*Ibid.*

[6]Herodotus, Papyrus Ebers II, quoted in E. A. Wallis Budge, *op. cit.*, pp. 177-178.

[7]Ange-Pierre Leca, *op. cit.*, p. 143.

[8]*Ibid.*, p. 144.

[9]Papyrus Sallier III, quoted in Ange-Pierre Leca, *op. cit.*, p. 138.

[10]Ange-Pierre Leca, *Ibid.*, p. 138.

[11]Barbara Mertz, *Red Land, Black Land* (New York: Dell Publishing Co., 1966), p. 317.

[12]*Ibid.*

[13]James Hamilton-Patterson and Carol Andrews, *op. cit.*, p. 44.

[14]A. T. Sandison, "The Use of Natron in Mummification in Ancient Egypt," *Journal of Near Eastern Studies*, XXII:4 (Oct., 1963), p. 267.

[15]Barbara Mertz, *op. cit.*, p. 314.

[16]Herbert Winlock, "The Tombs of the Kings of the Seventeenth Dynasty at Thebes," *Journal of Egyptian Archaeology*, X (1924), pp. 248-249.

[17]Barbara Adams, *op. cit.*, p. 41.

[18]James Hamilton-Patterson and Carol Andrews, *op. cit.*, p. 75.

[19]*Ibid.*, p. 79.

[20]*Ibid.*, p. 61.

[21]G. Frederick Owen, *Archaeology and the Bible* (Westwood, N.J.: Fleming H. Revell Co., 1961), p. 183.

[22]"Secrets Cooked from a Mummy," *Life* (Nov. 15, 1963), pp. 65-68.

[23]James Baikie, *Egyptian Papyri and Papyrus-Hunting*, p. 206.

Chapter 5

[1]James E. Harris and Kent R. Weeks, *X-Raying the Pharaohs* (New York: Charles Scribner's Sons, 1973), pp. 173-174. The full technical report on this project appears in James E. Harris and F. E. Wente (editors), *An X-Ray Atlas of the Royal Mummies* (Chicago: University Press, 1980).

[2]*Ibid.,* p. 174.

[3]James E. Harris and Kent R. Weeks, *op. cit.,* p. 122.

[4]*Ibid.,* p. 120.

[5]*Ibid.*

[6]A recently unwrapped mummy dated to 170 B.C. was also found to be uncircumcised. See Aidan Cockburn, Robin Barraco, Theodore Reyman and William Peck, "Autopsy of an Egyptian Mummy," *Science* CLXXXVII: 4182 (March, 1975), p. 1156.

[7]James E. Harris and Kent R. Weeks, *op. cit.,* p. 30.

[8]*Ibid.,* p. 34.

[9]*Ibid.,* p. 36.

[10]Aidan Cocburn, et el., *op. cit.,* p. 1155.

[11]See Robert S. Bianchi, "Egyptian Mummies: Myth and Reality, *Archaeology,* XXXV:2 (1982), p. 23. For a more complete report of this project see A. R. David (editor), *Mysteries of the Mummies* (Book Club Associates, 1978) and The *Manchester Project* (Manchester: Manchester University Press, 1979).

[12]Robert S. Bianchi, *op. cit.,* p. 23.

[13]Aidan Cockburn, et. el., *op. cit.,* p. 1155.

[14]*Ibid.,* p. 1156.

[15]*Ibid.*

[16]Jan C. Snow, "Mummy's the Word," *Beacon* (Dec. 30, 1984), pp. 12-15.

[17]*Ibid.,* p. 14.

[18]Thomas J. Pettigrew, *A History of Egyptian Mummies* (London: Longman, Rees, Orme, Brown, Green, and Longman, 1834), reprinted by North American Archives, Los Angeles, p. 7.

[19]*Ibid.,* p. 9.

[20]*Ibid.*, p. 8.

[21]James E. Harris and Kent R. Weeks, *op. cit.*, p. 92.

Chapter 6

[1]See James R. Battenfield, "A Consideration of the Identity of the Pharaoh of Genesis 47," *Journal of the Evangelical Theological Society*, XV: part II (1972), pp. 77-85.

[2]*Ibid.*, pp. 84-85.

[3]Charles F. Aling, *Egypt and Bible History* (Grand Rapids: Baker Book House, 1981), p. 31.

[4]*Ibid.*, p. 32.

[5]*Ibid.*

[6]*Ibid.*, pp. 34-52 and James R. Battenfield, *op. cit.*, pp. 77-85.

[7]Charles F. Aling, *op. cit.*, pp. 34-35.

[8]Francis Brown, S. R. Driver and Charles Briggs, *A Hebrew and English Lexicon of the Old Testament* (Oxford: The Clarendon Press, Corrected Impression, 1952), p. 179.

[9]*Ibid.*, p. 334.

[10]E. A. Wallis Budge, *op. cit.*, p. 179.

[11]*An Egyptian Mummy* (Melbourne, Australia: The Australian Institute of Archaeology, n.d.), pp. 6-7.

[12]*Ibid.*, p. 7.

[13]See discussion in James Hamilton-Patterson and Carol Andrews, *op. cit.*, p. 43.

[14]*Ibid.*, p. 43. Also see Alfred Lucas, *Ancient Egyptian Materials and Industries*, rev. J. R. Harris (New York: St. Martin's Press, 1962).

[15]See "The Story of Si-Nuhe," trans. by John A. Wilson, ANET, p. 21.

Bibliography

Books

Alred, E. *Egypt to the End of the Old Kingdom.* London: Thames and Hudson, 1965.

Alred, Cyril. *The Egyptians.* New York: Frederick A. Praeger, 1961.

Aling, Charles F. *Egypt and Bible History.* Grand Rapids: Baker Book House, 1981.

Allen, T. G. *The Book of the Dead.* Chicago: University of Chicago Press, 1974.

Andrews, Carol. *Egyptian Mummies.* Cambridge, Mass.: Harvard University Press, 1984.

Baikie, James. *A Century of Excavation in the Land of the Pharaohs.* London: Religious Tract Society, 1924.

_____ . *Egyptian Papyri and Papryus Hunting.* New York: Fleming H. Revell Company, n.d.

Belzoni, G. *Narrative of the Operations and Recent Discoveries within the Pyramids, Temples, Tombs, and Excavations in Egypt and Nubia.* London: Murray 1820.

Bierbrier, Morris. *The Tomb-Builders of the Pharaohs.* New York: Charles Scribner's Sons, 1982.

Bratton, Fred Gladstone. *A History of Egyptian Archaeology.* New York: Thomas Y. Crowell Company, 1968.

Breasted, James H. *Ancient Records of Egypt.* New York: Russell & Russell, 1962, reprint of 1906.

Brown, Francis; Driver, S. R.; and Briggs, Charles. *A Hebrew and English Lexicon of the Old Testament.* Oxford: The Clarendon Press, Corrected Impression, 1952.

Brunton, W. M. *Kings and Queens of Ancient Egypt.* London: Hodder and Stoughton, 1926.

Budge, E. A. W. *Egyptian Magic.* London: Trubner and Co., 1899.

Carter, H. *The Tomb of Tutankhamen.* 3 vols. New York: Cooper Square Publishers, Inc., reprinted 1963.

Ceram, C. W. *Gods, Graves and Scholars*. Trans. by E. B. Garside. London: Gollancz, Sidgwick and Jackson, 1952.

Cerny, Jaroslav. *Ancient Egyptian Religion*. New York: Hillary House, 1957.

Clark, S. and Englebach, R. *Ancient Egyptian Masonry*. London: Oxford University Press, 1930.

Cockburn, A. and E. *Mummies, Diseases and Ancient Cultures*. Cambridge: Cambridge University Press, 1983.

Cottrell, Leonard. *The Lost Pharaohs*. London: Evans, 1962.

David, Rosalie A., ed. *The Manchester Museum Mummy Project*. Manchester: Manchester Museum, 1979.

Davies, Norman de Garis. *The Tomb of Rekhmire at Thebes*. New York: Metropolitan Museum of Art, 1943.

Davis, John J. *Moses and the Gods of Egypt*. Grand Rapids: Baker Book House, 1971, revised, 1986.

_____ . *Paradise to Prison*. Grand Rapids: Baker Book House, 1975.

Davis, Theodore M. *The Tomb of Thutmosis IV*. London: Constable, 1904.

Dawson, Warren R. and Gray, P. H. K. *Catalogue of Egyptian Antiquities in the British Museum. I Mummies and Human Remains*. London: The Trustees of the British Museum, 1968.

deBuck, A. *The Egyptian Coffin Texts*. 7 vols. Chicago: University of Chicago Press, 1935-62.

Desroches-Noblecort, E. *Life and Death of a Pharaoh*. London: Penguin, 1965.

Disher, M. Wilson. *Pharaoh's Fool*. London: Heinemann, 1957.

Edwards, I. E. S. *The Pyramids of Egypt*. Baltimore: Penguin Books, 1954.

Emery, Walter B. *Archaic Egypt*. Baltimore: Penguin Books, 1961.

_____ . *Excavations at Sakkara: the Tomb of Hemaka*. Cairo: Government Press, 1938.

Erman, Adolf, ed. *The Ancient Egyptians*. New York: Harper and Row, 1966.

Fleming, S. and O'Conner, D. *The Egyptian Mummy: Secrets and Science*. Pennsylvania: The University Museum, 1980.

Frankfort, Henri. *Ancient Egyptian Religion.* New York: Harper and Brothers, 1961.

_____ . *Kingship and the Gods.* Chicago: The University of Chicago Press, 1948.

Gardiner, A. H. *Attitude of the Ancient Egyptians toward Death and the Dead.* Cambridge: University Press, 1935.

Gardiner, A. H. and Sethe, K. *Egyptian Letters to the Dead.* London: Egyptian Exploration Society, 1928.

Gardiner, Alan. *Egypt of the Pharaohs.* Oxford: The Clarendon Press, 1961.

Garstang, J. *Burial Customs of Ancient Egypt.* London: Constable, 1907.

Glanville, S. R. K. ed. *The Legacy of Egypt.* London: Oxford University Press, 1942.

Glob, P. V. *The Bog People.* Translated by Rupert Bruce-Mitford. Ithaca, N.Y.: Cornell University Press, 1969.

Grinsell, L. *Egyptian Pyramids.* Gloucester: John Bellows, Ltd., 1947.

Hamilton-Patterson, James and Andrews, Carol. *Mummies: Death and Life in Ancient Egypt.* New York: Penguin Books, 1978.

Harris, James E. and Weeks, Ken R. *X-raying the Pharaohs.* New York: Charles Scribner's Sons, 1973.

Harris, J. E. and Wente, E. F. (editors). *An X-ray Atlas of the Royal Mummies.* Chicago: University of Chicago Press, 1980.

Hayes, W. C. *The Sceptre of Egypt.* 2 vols. Cambridge, Mass: Harvard University Press, 1953-1959.

James, T. G. H. *Pharaoh's People.* London: The Bodley Head, 1984.

Kees, Hermann. *Ancient Egypt.* Chicago: University of Chicago Press, 1961.

Laver, J. P. *Saqqara: The Royal Cemetery of Memphis.* London: Thames and Hudson, 1976.

Leca, Ange-Pierre. *The Egyptian Way of Death.* translated by Louise Asmal. Garden City, N.Y.: Doubleday and Company, 1981.

Lesko, L. H. *The Ancient Egyptian Book of Two Ways.* Los Angeles: University of California Press, 1972.

Lieberman, Archie and Bradbury, Ray. *The Mummies of Guana-juato.* New York: Harry N. Abrams, 1974.

Lucas, A. *Ancient Egyptian Materials and Industries.* 4th ed., Revised and enlarged by J. B. Harris. London, 1962.

Martin, Richard A. *Mummies.* Chicago: Chicago Natural Museum Press, 1945.

Mercer, S. A. B. *The Religion of Ancient Egypt.* London: Luzac and Co., Ltd., 1949.

Mertz, Barbara. *Red Land, Black Land.* New York: Dell Publishing Co., 1966.

Montet, Pierre. *Egypt and the Bible.* Translated by Leslie R. Keylock. Philadelphia: Fortress Press, 1968.

_____ . *Eternal Egypt.* Translated by George Weidenfeld and Nicolson, Ltd., New York: The New American Library, 1964.

_____ . *Everyday Life in Egypt.* New York: Greenwood Press, 1974.

Murray, M. A. *The Tomb of Two Brothers.* Manchester, England: Manchester Museum Publications, No. 18, 1910.

Naville, E. *Cemeteries of Abydos,* I. London: Egypt Exploration Society, 1914.

Neubert, Otto. *Tutankhamen and the Valley of the Kings.* New York: Granada Publishing, Inc., 1977.

Owen, G. Frederick. *Archaeology and the Bible.* Westwood, N.J.: Fleming H. Revell Co.

Peet, T. E. *The Great Tomb Robberies.* London: Oxford University Press, 1940.

Pettigrew, Thomas J. *A History of Egyptian Mummies.* London: Longman, Rees, Orme, Brown, Green, and Longman, 1834. Reprinted by North American Archives, Los Angeles, n.d.

Posener, Georges. *Dictionary of Egyptian Civilization.* New York: Tudor Publishing Co., 1959.

Pritchard, James B., ed. *Ancient Near Eastern Texts.* Princeton: Princeton University Press, 1955.

Reisner, G. A. *The Development of the Egyptian Tomb Down to the Accession of Cheops.* Cambridge: Harvard University Press, 1936.

Romer, John. *Ancient Lives.* New York: Holt, Rinehart and Winston, 1984.

Smith, G. E. and Dawson, W. R. *Egyptian Mummies.* London: George Allen and Unwin, Ltd., 1924.

Smith, J. C. *Tombs, Temples and Ancient Art.* Norman, Okla.: University of Oklahoma Press, 1958.

Spencer, A. J. *Death in Ancient Egypt.* New York: Penguin Books, 1982.

Steindorff, George and Seele, Keith C. *When Egypt Ruled the East.* Chicago: The University of Chicago Press, 1957.

Wilson, John A. *The Culture of Ancient Egypt.* Chicago: The University of Chicago Press, 1951.

Winlock, Herbert E. *Materials Used at the Embalming of King Tutankhamen.* New York, 1941. reprinted by Arno Press, 1973.

_____ . *The Rise and Fall of the Middle Kingdom in Thebes.* New York: MacMillan, 1947.

_____ . *The Slain Soldiers of Nebhepetre Mentuhotpe.* New York: MacMillan, 1945.

Ziock, Hermann. *Guide to Egypt.* Cairo: Lehnert and Landrock, 1962.

Articles

Baer, K. "An Eleventh Dynasty Farmer's Letters to his Family." *Journal of American Oriental Society* LXXXIII (1963).

Battenfield, James. "A Consideration of the Identity of the Pharaoh of Genesis 47." *Journal of the Evangelical Theological Society.* XV. Part II (Spring, 1972).

Bianchi, Robert S. "Egyptian Mummies: Myth and Reality." *Archaeology,* XXXV, No. 2 (1982).

Blackman, A. M. "Oracles in Ancient Egypt." *The Journal of Egyptian Archaeology,* XII (1926).

Capart, J. and Gardiner, A. H. and van de Walle, B. "New Light on the Ramesside Tomb Robberies." *The Journal of Egyptian Archaeology.* XXII (1936), pp. 169-193.

Cockburn, Aidan. "Death and Disease in Ancient Egypt." *Science* CLXXXI, No. 4098 (August 1973).

Cockburn, Aidan and Barraco, Robin. "Autopsy of an Egyptian Mummy." *Science,* CLXXXVII No. 4182 (March 1975).

Connoly, R. C. "Kinship of Semenkhkare and Tut-Ankh-Amen Demonstrated." *Nature,* CCIV (1969).

David, A. R. "The Manchester Mummy Project," *Archaeology* XXXVIII; No. 6 (Nov/Dec., 1985).

Dawson, W. R. "Making a Mummy." *Journal of Egyptian Archaeology* XII (1927).

Dyson, Stephen L. "The Mummy of Middletown." *Archaeology* XXXII (1979).

Granville, A. B. "An Essay on Egyptian Mummies with Observations on the Art of Embalming among the Ancient Egyptians," *Philosophical Transactions of the Royal Society,* London (1825).

Green, M. A. "The Passing of Harmose." *Orientalia.* XLV, No. 4 (1976).

Gunn, B. "The Religion of the Poor in Ancient Egypt." *The Journal of Egyptian Archaeology* III (1961).

Harrison, R. G. and Abdalla, A. B. "The Remains of Tutankhamen." *Antiquity* XLVI: 181 (March, 1972).

Harrison, R. G. Connolly, R. C. and Abdalla, A. "Kingship of Semkhare and Tutankhamen Demonstrated Serologically." *Nature* CCIV (1969).

Leek, F. F. "Bread of the Pharaoh's Baker." *Newsletter of the American Research Center in Egypt* (April, 1971).

Murray, M. A. "Burial Customs and Beliefs in the Hereafter in Predynastic Egypt." *Journal of Egyptian Archaeology,* XLII, No. 86 (1956).

Radcliffe, Robert C. "South American Mummies Reveal 'Modern Diseases'." *The South Bend Tribune,* Nov. 30, 1980.

Sandison, A. T. "The Use of Natron in Mummification in Ancient Egypt." *Journal of Near Eastern Studies* XXII (1963).

Snow, Jan C. "Mummy's the Word." *Beacon,* Dec. 30, 1984.

Weigall, Arthur. "The Mummy of Akhenaton," *Journal of Egyptian Archaeology.* VIII (1922).

Wilson, J. A. "The Artist of the Egyptian Old Kingdom." *Journal of Near Eastern Studies,* VI, No. 231 (1947).

Winlock, Herbert, "The Tombs of the Kings of the Seventeenth Dynasty at Thebes," *Journal of Egyptian Archaeology,* X (1924).

Indices

Abbott Papyrus, 46
Aesculapius, 56
Akh, 28
Akhu, 29
Aling, Charles, 121
Amenemhet I, 19,21,32,35
Amenhotep III, 71,72
Amherst Papyrus, 49
Amset, 88
Amun, 49
Ani, 31,32
Antarctica, 76
Anubis, 31,94
Apis, 97,98

Ba, 25,27,29,76
Battenfield, James, 120
Belzoni, Giovanni Battista,
    15,17,69
Bilban el Hareem, 67
Bilban el Muluk, 67
Book of the Dead,
    31,32,36,67,92,94
Bratton, Fred, 46
British Museum,
    31,38,105,126
Brodkey, Jerald S., 115

Canopic box, 34,101
Canopic jars,
    78,82,88,99,102,113
Canopus, 100
Carter, Howard, 14,21
China, 84
City of the Dead, 46,67
City of the Living, 46
Coffin Texts, 31,67,80

Dahsur, 64
David, A. Rosalie, 112
Deir el Bahri,
    19,21,25,66,69,80,111
Diodorus, 82
Dorset Evening Echo, 12
Dre Abul Nega, 66

Egypt, Middle Kingdom,
    32,35,64,66,78,80,103
    106,120,121,122,123,128
Egypt, New Kingdom, 35,64
    67,69,80,84,90,94,105
Egypt, Old Kingdom, 27,55
    58,67,103
Egypt, Pre-dynastic period
    26,50,51,73
Egypt, 1st dynasty, 26,29,47
    48,50,52,53,54,77
——, 2nd dynasty, 26,46
    50,55,77
——, 3rd dynasty, 55,56
    57,77,101
——, 4th dynasty, 60,64
    78,92
——, 5th dynasty, 29,43
    78,101
——, 6th dynasty, 29,43
    45,64
——, 7th dynasty, 95
——, 10th dynasty, 95
——, 11th dynasty, 80,90
    92,95
——, 12th dynasty, 34,64
    92,95
——, 13th dynasty, 65,95
——, 17th dynasty, 95,111

____, 18th dynasty, 19,21
    37,50,67,126
____, 19th dynasty, 69,72
    94,95
____, 20th dynasty, 46,68
    95
____, 21st dynasty, 19,20,79
    80,81,82,90,94,101
____, 22nd dynasty, 43,82
    95
____, 23rd dynasty, 82
____, 26th dynasty, 82,94
    95,102
____, 30th dynasty, 95
Egypt, 1st Intermediate
    period, 64,78,80
Egyptian Museum (Cairo),
    69,71,92,108,117
Elmager, 111
Emery, Walter, 12,14
Evelyn-White, Hugh, 14

Fayuum, 64
Florence (Italy), 58
Frankfort, Henri, 27
Francois I, 111

Ghoran, 98
Giza, 42,55,56,58,59,60
    61,94
Graubelle (Jutland), 76
Great Britain, 12
Great Pyramid, 62
Greek(s), 70,72
Guanajuato (Mexico), 76

Haraldskjaer (Denmark), 76
Harris, James, 92,111
Hatshepsut, 66

Herodotus, 61,82,83,85,89
    126
Horus, 88,102
Hyksos, 108,120,122

Ibis, 28,31
Imhotep, 56
Iskander, Zaki, 127

Jacob, 123,128
Jones, Archibald, 11,12
Joseph, 119,120,122,123
    127, 128

Ka, 27,28,38,106
Karnak, 25
Khnum, 28,31
Khufu (Cheops), 58,61
Knet, 27

Leca, Ange-Pierre, 84
Lisht, 64
Loret, V., 21
Lucas, Alfred, 126
Lybian desert, 56

Manchester Museum, 112
Manetho, 120
Mariette, Auguste, 97
Maspero, Gaston, 18,19,108
Mastabas, 41,55,56,57
Memphis, 97
Menander, 99
Mendelssohn, Kurt, 62
Menkaure, 60,92,94
Mertz, Barbara, 87
Metropolitan Museum, 80
Milan (Italy), 58

Muu, 34,35

Nebseni, 105
Necropolis, 45,66,67
Nenki, 45
Nile, 32,46,58,62,70,100,106
    107
Nu, 38
Nubkhas, 49

Osiris, 43,46,94,100,106
Owen, G. Frederick, 97

Paser, 46,49
Petrie, Sir William Matthew
Flinders, 61
Pharaohs, 14,21,36,67,106
    122
Ptah, 91,97,105
Ptolemies, 69,92
Pyramids, 41,43,56,57,58,60
Pyramid texts, 29,31,67,80

Qebehsenuf, 88
Quibell, J.E., 77

Ramses II, 22,71,97,115
Re, 64,120
Roman(s), 70,92

Sakkara, 45,77
Sandison, A.T., 89
Sem priest, 35
Seti I, 19,69,72
Sinuhe, 35,128
Smith, Elliot, 108
Solomon, 120

Stenger-Philippe, Caroline,
    14

Tao, Seqenenre, 108,111
Thebes, 18,19,34,37,44,46
    66,67,108
Thoth, 31,32,98
Thutmose III, 13,22
Tollund (Jutland), 74-76
Tutankhamon, 14,50,92

Unis, 43
Ushabti, 102,103,105,106

Valley Chapel, 60
Valley of the Kings, 17,18
    19,21,67
Valley of the Queens, 67

Wilson, John A., 58
Wintlock, Herbert, 91
Wisdom of Anii, 43

Zoser, 56,57

Scripture Index

Genesis	1:26	23
	37:36	120
	39:2-3	122
	41:14	122
	41:38-44	122
	43:32	122
	46:34	122
	50	123,124
	50:2	119,124
	50:3	88,119,124
	50:24-25	127
	50:26	127
Exodus	12:40	120
	13:19	128
Joshua	24:32	128
Ruth	1:17	128
I Kings	6:1	120
II Kings	5:17	128
Hebrews	11:22	127